Heavenly Letters from Mum:

Daisy Gerda André

Anne Noëlette André

BALBOA.
PRESS

A DIVISION OF HAY HOUSE

Balboa Press books may be ordered through booksellers or by contacting:

Balboa Press
A Division of Hay House
1663 Liberty Drive
Bloomington, IN 47403
www.balboapress.com
1 (877) 407-4847

Because of the dynamic nature of the Internet, any web addresses or
links contained in this book may have changed since publication and
may no longer be valid. The views expressed in this work are solely those
of the author and do not necessarily reflect the views of the publisher,
and the publisher hereby disclaims any responsibility for them.

The author of this book does not dispense medical advice or prescribe the use
of any technique as a form of treatment for physical, emotional, or medical
problems without the advice of a physician, either directly or indirectly. The
intent of the author is only to offer information of a general nature to help
you in your quest for emotional and spiritual well-being. In the event you use
any of the information in this book for yourself, which is your constitutional
right, the author and the publisher assume no responsibility for your actions.

Any people depicted in stock imagery provided by Thinkstock are
models, and such images are being used for illustrative purposes only.
Certain stock imagery © Thinkstock.

Print information available on the last page.

ISBN: 978-1-4525-2914-1 (sc)
ISBN: 978-1-4525-2915-8 (e)

Balboa Press rev. date: 06/15/2015

Contents

In loving memory of my lovely and beautiful mum, Daisy Gerda André (February 8, 1928–May 29, 2003), and to my two adorable children: Mary Rosa Caroline St. Louis and Michaël Loïc St. Louis. I want you both to be proud of your mum always, as I was always proud of mine.

Acknowledgements

I give special thanks to my close sister Monique Godefroy, who sent me a book on automatic/spirit writings. It instantly awakened my inner desires and inspiration.

I also wish to thank my other siblings, Majo, Arlette, Sylvain, (in the spirit world) and Jacqueline, Mireille, Neils, Michel and Angélique and my nieces, nephews, cousins, and extended members of Mum's family (still all living). And special thanks to my dearest goddaughter Delphine.

Last but not least, special thanks go to the mediums Joanne King (Australia) (author of *Nobody Will Ever Believe You*), Franc de Paris (France), Eliot Moussa (Algeria) and Neale Donald Walsch of the book series *Conversations with God* 1997–2005, upon which the 2006 movie of the same name was based. My gratitude also goes to Corinne Pialle, author of *Instants Magiques* (Broché-2002); Fathers Adrien Wiehé and Jean Maurice Labour (Mauritius); my ex-husband, Louis Jean Noël St. Louis; and my best friend, Tony Monea for always encouraging me to go ahead with the publishing.

Divine love, light, healings and endless blessings,

Anne Noëlette André

Preface

To all souls on earth who have lost someone dear to their heart and who need to know if their loved ones are still alive and around them, may you find relief and peace in these pages. Do not be sad. Your loved ones on the other side—in the other dimensions—are near you. As long as they exist in your heart, they don't depart. Talk to them, and they will communicate with you through thoughts that come when your mind is silent. They are talking to you there continuously, so respond to them. Tune yourself to a higher frequency; they will adjust themselves to a lower frequency, and you will meet in between your natural levels.

Close your eyes, clear your mind of daily thoughts, think of your loved ones, and as you do the aforementioned frequency changes, you will connect with each other. Put some music on, as it raises vibrations, and it might help you to meditate and go deep within yourself. Feel your loved ones around you, as they never really left. We are all energy, and energy never dies. We are also vibrations. Through our vibrations, we can direct ourselves toward them and ask them whatever we need to know. They are waiting for us to talk to them. Trust your inner self, surrender, and wait for magic to take place.

Don't cry on the graves of your loved ones. They are not there! They are right beside you, behind you, in front of you, above you, and in you.

May you experience divine love, light, healings, and blessings, now and always.

Anne Noëlette André

DAISY GERDA ANDRÉ

I wish a happy, peaceful, and spiritual reading experience to all. May you find peace, comfort, closure, and answers here. More importantly, I hope you find light, truth, and love through proof of an afterlife. Open yourself in silence, and let love guide you to those you hold dear who have passed from this life. Beyond the veil, much love exists, so listen to their call. If you think that life is not worth living, give me a chance to prove you wrong. Wait to decide until after you go on my inspirational journey. There is a reason you are reading this: you've been chosen for a new journey. Congratulations!

Peace, light, and love to you.

Anne Noëlette André

Synopsis

HOW IT ALL BEGINS

Mum left her physical body in this dimension on May 29, 2003. Nothing was really the same in our family or life afterward. So much sadness surrounded us. We were a family of ten children at first. Two passed to the other side very young: my brother Sylvain André, who was four months old and suffered from jaundice, and my sister Arlette André, who was two years old and suffered from heart issues. Six girls and two boys remained in the physical world. We were all devastated at Mum's funeral. Spiritual life after physical death had no real meaning to us.

I needed comfort; therefore, I read several books wherein people who had lost their loved ones connected with them by the method of automatic/spirit writings. I was intrigued and wanted to know more. Therefore, I decided to try it after I read that special book entitled *Instants Magiques* by Corinne Pialle. I have to thank my sister Monique for sending me the book from Paris.

I was quite sceptical of having any results. To my great surprise, I received several messages over five years until May

2008. Now, after seven years of silence from the time of the last message and after contact with several mediums over the years, telling me that I need to publish these lovely writings, I finally present them. I believed in the authenticity of these writings, but I stopped the practice because of some non-believers in my family. These family members discouraged me from continuing to communicate with my mum in the other dimension. However, after reading the messages again, I have no doubt that they were the truth, as evidence in such writings supported things that happened over the years after her physical death!

Therefore, after no fewer than four priests and five mediums told me that I should publish the writings, as they were meant to be shared with everyone on earth, here they are. Mum also told me to share them with everyone, but I hesitated after seeing the reactions to paranormal writings from members of my family. I did not want to look like a fool in front of society. However, now I look foolish for not publishing these beautiful writings. I should not have cared about people's opinions regarding my beliefs. I believed strongly in the written conversations Mum and I had over the years, and I should have listened to my intuition, my heart, and my soul.

My hope and prayer is that anyone who has lost someone close to their heart finds comfort while reading these pages and to know that it was not the end when their loved ones passed on, here on earth. Only their physical body died, as our etheric body (the energy fields around our physical body, or auras), our mind, and our soul never die. The etheric body gives health, life, and organization to the physical body. It attunes our consciousness to the principle of energy. It brings energies from the higher bodies down into our physical consciousness. Our astral bodies give us the ability to have desires, emotions, an imagination, and psychic abilities. The power they lend to our thoughts is essential for effective action and manifestation, and they never die.

We are each composed of energy, and energy never dies; therefore, our loved ones remain alive and well. We continue to exist, and we bring with us what we used to be physically and mentally. We can exist in any form, and thus we people will recognize us the way we were, but we will appear better than we could possibly imagine.

So, dear readers, your loved ones are the same as they used to be. Talk to them and they will answer you. They surround you every single day and protect you from danger and evil. Trust your instinct when it suggests that they are much closer to you than you would imagine. They still see you, talk to you, and hear you. Never forget them, as they are always around. They talk to you through your thoughts, now and always!

With love,

Anne Noëlette André

§§§

If I had to describe mum in one word, it would be giver, *as she always loved to share and give. There was always plenty of food on the table, and she wanted life to be like a daily party for everyone.*

Chapter 1

LEAVING THE PHYSICAL WORLD

On Wednesday, May 21, 2003, I received a phone call from Mum, telling me that she was going to die. I remember it well. She told me that she had been very sick and that my brother Michel and my sister Mireille were bringing her to the private hospital. Panicked, I left work immediately and joined them there. Mum walked to the doctor's office. No one would say that she was dying or that eight days later, she would be dead. It was clear that she was in pain, but not that it was fatal. However, the doctor did an electrocardiogram, and the result was a terrible shock to all of us: Mum had an acute myocardial infarction.

The doctors admitted Mum instantly. She was suffering badly. My sister, my brother, and I were speechless. We were aware that she had been suffering from chest pain since the previous Sunday, three days before. As she was a qualified nurse and a midwife and told us that it was only mild indigestion, we did not give great importance to the pain she was dealing with. We trusted what she said.

I now think that she did not want to face the truth that it could be something worse than an upset stomach. She would have known what was going on with her health as she was a nurse and has been working in hospitals for years. We didn't know better and we believed what she said and went along with her diagnosis, and we were all wrong. As I watched her lying on the bed in the intensive care unit at the clinic, she looked in my eyes and said, "I am going to die." She was in terrible pain, and we were helpless. As soon as she rested her body on the hospital bed, we could see how unwell she was.

The report felt like a sharp knife in our hearts: there was no hope. We contacted our other sisters—Marie Josée, Jacqueline, Angélique, and Monique (the latter both overseas)—and our other brother, Neils. They too were shocked at the announcement that Mum would leave us very soon. We had all experienced the loss of our dad three years earlier on July 16, 2000. We siblings could not believe that it was happening to our other parent so soon or accept the fact that Mum was so suddenly in such a deteriorated state. Other than the presumed indigestion that she complained of the past Sunday, she was a very healthy strong woman. She was still on her feet, doing everything by herself. The previous day, she had gone to the city market to buy her vegetables and meat. Our two overseas sisters, one on the island of Réunion and the other in France, decided to take the next flights possible to be with us in this difficult time.

The cardiologist explained that Mum had a big hole in her heart, and all we could do was wait. Mum still did not know the truth, as we did not tell her about the seriousness of her condition. She still thought that she had dyspepsia[1]. Alternatively, maybe she knew but did not want to face the fact that this was the end. If we had brought Mum to the clinic the day she told us about her indigestion, three days earlier, they could have done bypass surgery to save her, as she had only experienced a heart attack at that point. However, the infarction had caused too much damage since. We siblings grouped around Mum's bed in disbelief. Mum told us all that our last reunion would be around her cadaver, and she was right. On her third day at the clinic, the doctors told us that there was no hope. As we were devout Catholics, we called our local priest, Father Adrien Wiehé, from St. Louis Cathédrale to give her last communion.

The following Sunday, May 25, 2003, was Mother's Day. How painful it was for us to see our mum suffering on a day that should have been restful. It hurt us to see her dealing with so much pain and suffering, unable to enjoy the bouquet we got her. I brought my two children, Caroline and Loïc, to see her on that special day. This was the last time she saw them and received kisses from them. She was happy to have seen everyone. She cried for help. Even though she was on painkillers and morphine injections, she was in deep pain, and it was extremely hard for all of her children to watch her like that. For us, it was not a happy Mother's Day at all. It was, on the contrary, a day of suffering.

Two nights earlier, we had been laughing at her story of the goat and the chicken. She liked telling this funny tale to teach us the great moral to never to be 100 per cent sure of what's next—in other words, we should never presume things in life are going to turn out the way we expect. In this

---

[1]   Indigestion

story, a man had invited some guests to his house the next day, and his servants prepared to kill the goat and make a great dinner for the guests. When the chicken heard what was going on, it went to the goat and said, "Goat, this is going to be your last night. Tomorrow you are going to be killed, cooked, and eaten." The chicken made quite a scene of it and then went to sleep with complete peace of mind, dreaming about the goat being cooked. Meanwhile, the goat could not sleep all night and was having nightmares of people killing him. The next day, most of the guests excused themselves, and the man had no reason to kill the goat. He said to his servants, "Go get the chicken, and we'll make a good curry." When the goat heard this, it smiled at the chicken in relief, while the chicken was terrified.

When Mum told this story, her gestures and the tone of her voice made us laugh loudly. Oh, Mummy, I still can hear how you told the story so brightly. You had an uncommon sense of humour. I have always loved you and always will.

On Tuesday, May 27, 2003, we had surrounded Mum for seven consecutive days and nights. That day will forever remain in our collective memory, as she fell into a coma and lost contact with us. She was already halfway to the other side and not suffering anymore; she looked as if she was dreaming peacefully. All eight of her children were around her on the eighth night at the hospital, Wednesday, 28 May 2003. Mum was still in a coma, and the cardiologist told us that she would not make it through the night. We all expected her to pass over.

We were exhausted, but we wanted her to go in peace, as she had been through so much pain. We prayed for her all night, and we told her that it was all right for her to go.

We would be fine, so she could let go of everything and leave us with peace of mind. She passed over to other side at 1:25 a.m. on Friday, 29 May 2003, at the reputed private clinic in Port Louis, Mauritius Island, where she received care. She surrendered her three last breaths in front of my sisters Monique and Angélique and my brother Michel. Some of us siblings, including me, were resting our eyes when this occurred. We all jumped to our feet as Angélique and Monique called us into our mum's room. After her third long breath, she expired in front of my brother Michel, who was alone with her. When we reached her room, we all gathered around her as she passed to the other side. She looked peaceful and relieved. There was a little smile on her face and one last teardrop in her right eye.

She was herself again, in good health, young, happy, and surrounded by light and love from the spirit world. Our physical eyes could no longer see, hear, or feel her presence. We could only sense it if we raised ourselves to her level and she lowered herself to ours. We thought, "This is it. She is gone forever, and we will never be able to talk to her, hear her, or feel her again." However, we were all wrong!

She seemed really at peace and really happy. Her eyes were open, so my brother Neils closed them and told her to rest in peace. Her final tear fell. I helped two nurses clean Mum and dress her in funeral clothes. She had planned everything and told us what to wear before her death. It was so emotional for me to give my mum her last shower on this earth. What had happened paralysed us siblings. We felt lost without her by our side anymore. She always said that she was a pole for us, and once the pole is broken down, nothing would ever be the same. Oh how she was right! Looking back, I now realize how psychic Mum was.

Nothing was the same after that night. My siblings and I lost what she taught us about the value of family, and we lost our strong connection. She was always the right example of happy reunion. Through the years after her death, we lost our feeling of solidarity towards each other. All the care and love that she taught us is gone. To this day, there are misunderstandings and carelessness among the members of our family. We have not learned from this, unfortunately. Life is a gift, and we should all live in peace and harmony and love each other, as we could lose each other suddenly, but we seemingly did not learn this from our mum's death. Sadly, after Mum was gone, the unity went away with her. We, her children, should all be ashamed of this, but life goes on for each of us. I learn to let go and move on with my own life—my reason for being here. God did not mean for humans to stay live with their families or follow their family beliefs forever. Rather, we are each here to live our life and to be aware of our purpose. One day, when my siblings and I are older, maybe we will understand what we missed and why we held on to grudges against each other for so long. Every day, we each have a new chance to rectify our misunderstandings. May God and his angels heal us from any unforgiven things in our hearts. Everything is meant to be. If I did not go through this whole experience, I guess I would not be who I am today. I would not be writing this book. I hope that the contents will touch our hearts to let go, to forgive, and to heal from the past and of all the pain that we voluntarily or involuntarily caused each other.

§§§

My beautiful mum was so peaceful in her coffin. She was back at her house at three in the morning on 29 May 2003, and we organized her funeral at three the same afternoon. When Mum left her home the week before, she and we never imagined that she would return in a coffin. There were many flowers from families, friends, and colleagues, and she looked stunning in her two-piece dress and flowers in her hair. I needed to make her look beautiful, so I did her makeup and hair with great emotion. She looked younger and ready to go to a ball. "Oh my God, how wonderful you looked, Mum. I love you so much," I thought.

In the church, we siblings were united in spirit with our mum, and the priest said that she was still alive. How could we pay attention to him, as we knew we would no longer be able to hold her in our arms, talk to her, see her, or hear her? His words were like a soft breeze of hope, but some of us were not convinced that she heard or saw us—that only her physical body died, while her spirit was alive, watching us, surrounding us, and loving us.

We were blind to such magic, such truth, in that difficult time. It took time for some of us to understand that Mum was still alive and well, in a much better place, with no more pain and suffering. Nevertheless, we were dealing with the pain of her loss, so we could not immediately accept that she was safe and well and that we should be happy for her. It was so hard to accept the loss of someone we loved since the day we were born. Until we all accept that she is still near us, many of us will suffer pain, depression, anxiety, panic attacks, and endless sadness.

In peace, lovely angel, just fly.
Yes, just go to this wonderful place you always dreamed of
And that you were singing about to us on your last days
with us here.
Go towards this happiness, Mum.
Prepare the place for us until the day that will reunite us all
Around you again and happy expressing you our dearest love
Now, then, and always.
From this day,
We will be thinking when we wake up
That we might not see the fallen night.
In the evening, before we fell asleep,
That we might not see the following dawn.
May this thought help us live our lives better,
In perfect harmony with each other,
To harvest the fruit in our future life
The day we depart, at dawn or at sunset,
While leaving everything and everyone:
Our parents, siblings, family, children, friends, assets,
money—
Everything and everyone
To join those who left us
And also to be near our well-loved
Father, Son, and Holy Spirit, whom we must love above all,
And also Mary, the angels, and all the saints,
Who all expect us, back to the source
To taste the rewards that await us
For our lives humbly lived on earth.

—Anne Noëlette André

Chapter 2

THE FIRST MESSAGES

After Mum left us, days seemed endless. We were all depressed, as it was hard for us to accept that she was gone. A loved one who had been living with my mum before she passed over was especially suffering from depression. It was so painful. I was very depressed too, as every weekend before Mum's death, I used to go to her house with my two children: Caroline, my daughter, aged nine, and Loïc, my son, aged three. Afterward, it was hard for me to head down there to an empty house, although I felt her presence everywhere inside the residence. It was so awkward. I was into all sorts of things that helped me believe that she was still around. I convinced myself that she was still nearby.

My lovely sister Monique sent me books from Paris about the afterlife and told me about special books on a spirit communication technique. I read all of them, but one particularly had all my attention, as it described written communication between a son who had passed over and his mum. Moreover, it was a written communication. They called it "automatic writings"[2] or "spirit writings," one of many possibilities of mediumship. I did not know this existed or if it could possibly work. I was quite sceptical, but I was also very impressed by the conversations they had in writing. In addition, I felt relieved when I read how happy the woman was to hear from her passed-on son again. Every day and night, she did not miss a chance to have contact with him. And then I thought, "I believe that if two souls love each other deeply, their feelings should remain same for each other even if one of them died physically. If love itself is eternal, so are we all spiritually. Therefore, such communication could happen if both parties believed in such unconditional love after physical death." Moreover, as we all know, we are all energy, and energy never dies. Therefore, I was ready to believe this evidence of such communication, and I decided to give it a go.

I felt driven to try automatic/spirit writings on June 29, 2003, exactly one month after my mum passed over. I was at work in my private office, and something (a thought) or someone (Mum or my spirit guide) in my mind constantly told me to try it. I thought that if someone entered my office and saw me doing it, they would think I was crazy. I did not believe that I was good enough to communicate with someone in the spirit world. However, I felt motivated to try, so I took a piece of blank white paper and a pen. That is all you need. I closed my eyes for a couple minutes and asked my mum, inside my heart, to come talk to me. I brushed away distractions and opened my mind to any thoughts that were not my imagination. I did not expect anything to

---

[2]   A spirit communication technique

happen. However, I gave it a go. I asked a simple question first, guided by the book I read: "Mum, are you in heaven?"

I waited patiently for an answer. My hand stood still, holding the pen on the paper. Suddenly, to my big surprise, my hand started to move and writings appeared on the page, but I could not understand a word of it. I let my hand write whatever it wanted to compose. My hand stopped suddenly. I was very intrigued, as I felt that some inexplicable force had controlled my hand. I asked another question, waited patiently, and my hand started writing illegible things again. I kept asking questions, and my hand kept writing. I had no idea what I had written. And then there were no more answers. If you want to put it another way, my hand stopped responding to the questions I asked. I thought the spirit, or unknown force, was gone. I did not yet have confirmation that it was my mum. I looked at the page for a moment and did not understand anything. I looked closer, and then I saw some words that I could easily read. I separated the words that I saw, as explained in the book I had read. It was like a chain of words, so I had to separate them by putting a dash between each one, making it more readable. You can see a French sample of my first automatic/spirit writings, translated into English on the following pages. Indeed, I speak, read and write French and English. My third language is Creole; the written communications were all in French, my preferred language.

Maman es tu au ciel ?

~~(illisible)~~

Es tu heureuse ?

~~(illisible)~~

Tu nous manques tant, tu sais.

~~(illisible)~~

Maman je t'aime, tu sais ?

~~(illisible)~~

On a du mal à accepter ton départ ?

...merait bien te voir à la maison
d on y va, la maison est tellement
sans toi.

~~illegible scribble~~

an nous sommes de nouveau tranquil,
peux continuer ou alors dois tu
ir ???

~~illegible scribble~~

t'aime fort maman
is tes enfants te regrettent
t'aiment très fort.

~~illegible scribble~~
brasses Dieu, Jesus et Marie pour moi.

Spirit Writings: June 29, 2003 (First Attempt); Start Time 9:00 a.m. End Time 10:15 a.m.

Me: Mum, are you in heaven?

Mum: Yes, I am in heaven.

Me: Are you happy?

Mum: Yes, I am happy.

Me: We miss you so much, you know?

Mum: I am with you always. Your mum is with you forever. I am with you every day.

Me: Mum, we love you. Do you know that?

Mum: The same way I love you. Mum will always love you.

Me: It's hard for us to accept that you are gone.

Mum: Mum is with you now, and I am really your mum, who will love you always.

Me: We would have liked seeing you home when we go there; the house is so empty without you there.

Mum: You are in my heart, and I love you. I need to go, but I will return each time you write to me.

Me: I love you, Mum. All your children miss you and love you so much.

Mum: I love you too, so much.

Me: Kiss God, Jesus, and Mother Mary for me.

Mum: I thank you.

Chapter 3

DEALING WITH THE SCEPTICS

"Oh my God, is this for real?" I thought. I had tears in my eyes while writing the message, as I was overwhelmed with emotion. I could not believe I was having a conversation with my mum in the spirit world. Wasn't this my imagination? I was happy and scared at the same time. Questions filled my head: What am I going to do? Do I have to tell the other members of my family what just happened? Will they believe this? They might either think I am going crazy because of my depressive state from losing Mum. I felt stupid when I predicted their reactions. I knew that I had to share this with my sisters and brothers, as Mum was talking to them too. I had the responsibility of passing the message on to them.

As I expected, some members of the family would not believe that I had received such communication. Some requested that I perform an automatic/spirit writings in front of them to prove it, and I did so when I went back to Mum's house, where we all gathered over the weekends. Others never believed in the writings and were not interested in reading the messages. The rest, on the other hand, believed that the messages could be true, but they only half believed that these messages came from our mum. I continued the communications. However, some of my siblings told me that I was in the wrong and disturbing Mum, who should be resting in peace. I thought, "You've got it all wrong. She is not resting at all. She is alive and well and busy doing things up there." Family members also told me to let her be with the dead and that I should be with the "living". They said that I was completely losing my mind; I needed to focus on my life and my family and stop these communications. In retrospect, I think that we are the ones who are "dead", as we cannot see, hear, or sense clearly, while the ones who passed over are living, as they see everything differently but clearly at a level of consciousness beyond what we could ever imagine.

I felt lost, but some family members encouraged me to continue, and I did despite the doubts in my mind. I was confused, but I did not want to end this wonderful experience yet. They were priceless moments. Nobody understood the emotions I experienced through such communications; these feelings changed my overall perception of life itself and made me feel a heavy responsibility to pass them on to the recipients who would not likely accept them. I had to experience the ridicule of feeling like a fool each time I got a message. How could they see me as normal when I was telling my family that our dead mum was communicating to us through automatic/spirit writings? It was hard when I saw their expressions of doubt and unresponsiveness. I wish it were easier to pass messages from those from the spirit world to those in the physical world, as people in 2003, the people close to me were far from believing that this was possible when love exists or the desire for it to happen makes it possible. Today, it's much easier, as people have evolved a lot in their awareness of eternal life.

It was hard work to read the messages from Mum and pass them along, as more and more kept coming. Some relatives had a stronger belief in them, but others still denied their legitimacy. Most importantly, I believed in them. I heard things at a spiritual level, and things appeared so beautiful and clear with my new perspective. If my family had experienced what I was experiencing, everything would have been much easier and things would be different today. However, I can't blame any of them. If I were in their place, I might not have believed myself. Therefore, I cannot judge their attitude or feelings about what was happening, and I could not pressure them to believe in something they did not want to believe. I knew they had free will, and I respected that.

Chapter 4

WE ARE DIVINE

Spirit Writings: June 30, 2003; Start Time 11:15 a.m. End Time 11:40 a.m.

Me: Mum, are you near me right now?

Mum: Mum is always near you all; Mum is in communion with you all.

Me: Mum, how do you feel up there? Describe how it is.

Mum: I am now in heaven. Mum will never forget you. Heaven is beautiful. I cannot describe its splendour, so endless. Yes, it is really so beautiful.

Me: Mum protects us from evil.

Mum: I will always protect you. Do not fear. I love you all.

Me: Mum, I need to go.

Mum: Goodbye.

Later on that same day …

Spirit Writings: June 30, 2003; Start Time 12:30 p.m. End Time 1:10 p.m.

Me: Mum, here I am again. Forgive me asking this, but what happened to your necklace?[3]

Mum: I lost my necklace on my way home. Note: it is better this way. I am sad too, but it is better that I lost it so that there is no jealousy. When we meet again, I will love you all. I see you all differently today, and I love you so much more. Love each other, as God will reward you one day in heaven. I have not stopped loving you or praying for you. Pray to the Holy Spirit; he will protect you against evil.

Mum used the phrase "no jealousy", as we knew that the necklace would go to a member of the family after Mum's physical death. I think that Mum was right saying that it was better that the necklace was lost, as everyone who did not get it might have felt hurt. This could have created even more friction in our family! A medium told me once that Mum had lost it in a taxi that she took home. Maybe it fell, and in her unwell state, she did not notice.

I asked Mum about the necklace again later, and she said, "I really lost it. It fell in front of me. Look ahead of you, Noëlette,[4] and not behind, as it is one thing among so many other superficial and material ones. Hold on to the spiritual things. Hold on to God, the light of this world where you are and where I am. He is our saviour."

The conversations increased and continued. I could not sleep anymore. I woke up in the middle of the night as if

---

[3]   There was a mystery around Mum's necklace disappearing. The necklace was 22 carats and it had a golden heart pendant that was so beautiful. It was very valuable.

[4]   My middle name.

something was awakening me. I had to get up, get my paper and pen in hand, and start writing. I could not live anymore without this conversation between Mum and me.

Some of the messages are quite personal to my brothers and sisters, and some are for all people. For the sake of privacy, I used fake names. It took me twelve years to do this because I let others decide for me. I let their doubts control me and discourage me from pursuing this magical form of communication with our mum. I regret letting my mum down when I stopped the daily conversations around May 2008. By now, she is probably in a much higher level of consciousness. Moreover, I have evolved too. I occasionally get another type of communication from beyond, mostly inspirational writings coming from my mind or from my spirit guide. I have no control over it; rather, my mind receives dictation, and I have to type the message without thinking. Automatic/Spirit writings was physical mediumship, [Tuning at higher frequencies consume your energies. You might feel quite tired after a session and it also affect your emotions knowing you are receiving messages from beyond]. Now I can hear the spirit like an inner voice. This type of communication is known as mental mediumship. I never knew before Mum's death that I had such gifts, and never would have known it if Mum and I did not have these written conversations. I guess everything happens at the right place and the right time. Hence, the publication date of this book is no coincidence. I wish you, dear readers, great comfort, closure, hope, and certainty that you will meet your loved ones again to reunite in joy and happiness. You will embrace them again when the right time comes. Never doubt this. They will wait for you as you get back into the source, our real home—paradise.

Inspirational Spirit Writings: March 16, 2014, Anne André

Whatever you believe in which is goodness is love;
Whatever you think of with good intention is love;
Whatever you look at with blessings is love;
Whatever you speak of with wisdom and care is love;
Whatever, with your hands, you heal is love;
Whatever your actions are made of which intends nothing in return is love;
Love attracts love,
So more and more actions and examples of love will just bring us more and more amazing experiences of love.

§§§

Channelling: March 19, 2014, Anne André

Recharge your batteries from energies from Mother Nature;
Breathe energies from power of the bright warm sun,
From a bright full moon,
From just watching the infinite bright stars at night,
From getting you lost in the endless sky,
From the energetic trees,
From the beautiful colourful flowers and smell,
From the various energized plants,
From the sea and its waves which come and go and clean the shore again and again,
From the walk in a vast forest,
From watching the beautiful landscape of a valley,
From the strength you get visualizing the climbing of a mountain,
From the water running from a cascade,

From the beautiful singing tunes and vibrations of the lovely birds,
From water running from a river and merging into the sea,
From the various stones and especially all types of crystals.
Yes, breathe in all energies to heal and balance your etheric fields;
Breathe in, yes, all good, positive energies you have freely from nature,
And breathe out all toxic ones from your physical body.
Have you ever thought about it?
Of these energies available freely to all of us to be healed, repeatedly, each new day!
Have a wonderful great day, filled with wonderful positive energies.

§§§

Inspirational Writings: July 12, 2014, Anne André

There is no separation in human race, colour, religion, culture, nature, animals, etc.… well, we are one with the universe. We are all the mirror of each other, meaning you are I; I am you; he is she; and she is he; we are them; and they are us. In other words, we are all the reflection of each other, all in us and us in all; therefore, we are unseparated, as we are us—one in all and all in one."

§§§

Channelling: January 9, 2015, Anne André

Be paradise on earth;
You are meant to reproduce it.
How proud are we of you all who are light workers in this dimension of yours.
We are always near you to guide you on the celestial path.
Hear us, we call upon you to hear us all the time.
How wonderful it is to work with you, through you, as you let us [to].
Be blessed as all your generation for being such a human angel and light worker and love worker in your dimension. We watch [on] you, and we bring you to where you are meant to be in your life's purpose.
Love, love, love is all that matters.
Show and give love to all without distinction.
Don't create barriers with religions, as all is one with the Almighty.
We love you all. No hate—peace and love.

§§§

Spirit Writing: January 10, 2015, Anne André

It is your year to come out of the closet, shine beautifully and make use of all your potentials—hidden or unused qualities. Yes, your time to sparkle like a brilliant star. Let go of the fear of not succeeding in your work, project, or career and in relationships. Be healed from the past and free yourself from all unforgiven situations and people who have hurt you or whom you've hurt. Be positive that you have everything in you to maintain a healthy life, remain fit physically, and be mentally balanced. Keep away from dramas—dramatic people or situations. Remain positive and have positive thoughts; by doing this, you create your immediate reality. Don't give anyone the power to hurt you. Protect yourself by calling upon Archangel Michael in any weak situation. Pray, ask, and you shall receive.

Love, light, blessings to you all.

§§§

Channelling: April 15, 2014, Anne André

"As the sun every morning with its light shines on you
Its gentleness touches your skin and makes you feel morally good as soon as you see it
And its heat warms your body and heart
You too every morning be a light for others.
Convey your light so that they too are illuminated like you.
Shines in all your lights and miles shipments of magic as a fairy
That her wand is of good wishes to all
You also transmit in all on your way.
You too be a every morning sweetness
Like honey in the mouth and warms your throat at all times.
Be that sweetness to others to illuminate their sad face
And put joy on their face and there in their mind and in their heart.
Rayons for those hoping to do more and who believe in such a gentle way of life.
You too be every morning an eternally renewed sun.
A sun that warms the other by your looks, your actions and words spoken or written
Yes that warms the hearts of so many others who are weakened by life.

Because of the disease, misery, famine, the unexpected
Contempt of others, their judgment, their hatred;
Yes You Be that sun for all.
Be the sun sky for the land.
On land you are our sunshine:
by your smile, because of your compassion, the love you give
without expecting anything in return.
by your humility before your own beauty, your own success;
by your simplicity in everything you make.
You are the Sun, one of our millions of small suns on earth
You are one of our millions of light that shines every day
Warming and enlightening those who have not hope for
their own sun.
For you are a sun that have the gift of shining and warming
But just some lost faith in their power.
But you are you are here, you exist to remind them
Be our sun, the sun from heaven to earth, now and forever."

§§§

Inspirational Writing: April 29, 2015, Anne André

"We came into this world naked, without anything,
innocent, fragile, white of all sins;
At that moment we knew nothing of differences in skin
color, religion, language, country, rich in knowledge of
power, money, material goods etc.
During our life, we are building ourselves all barriers,
All the prejudices and differences between colors, nations,
peoples, religions and languages;
We do not understand that everything is lent us down here;

And we'll have to leave everything to go back where we came from;
We came here to live happily in the love of our neighbor because that's our next us likewise, our own reflection.
For it has been said, *"I was hungry and you gave me to eat; I was sick and you visited me, I was thirsty and you gave me drink; I was without clothes and you clothed me."*[5]
So when we understand that the other, our neighbor, our friend, our enemy:
This is the Christ himself, as we are all in him and he in us all.
That there was no need to create as many useless barriers
Because soon we will have to go back to the source
Leaving everything and going back the same as we came."

§§§

Channelling: April 29, 2015, Anne André

"What it makes us happy to see you and work for heaven;
Reheating the sky by your gentleness, kindness, patience and tolerance;
Your determination to the task of being the lightworkers;
Your tiny lights everyone makes a huge light that illuminates the earth and the sky at the same time
And all other spaces and times.
You cannot imagine the beauty that you create;
If you knew that you would not even believe in your eyes
And yet know how much your efforts, your only task is recognized and appreciated.
Nothing you do is excluded; everything is seen and heard.

---

[5] Matthew 25:35-36

Know that we are proud of you for your continued efforts
To make your dimension serene, harmonious and peaceful
living.
Earthly Angels; Earth Angels; Angels of heaven; Lightworkers;
You are the instruments of peace, resolution of conflicts
and wars
And we protect you and guide you where you need to be to
accomplish your mission.
Have no fears, your guides, us, we are always at your side.
We will never leave you, as we inspire you to be what you are
And you hear us, that's why you understand more than others.
Share your knowledge, as simply as possible;
For all to understand the language you speak.
In simplicity, more are affected and understand.
Thank you to exist, thank you for understanding, thank you
for listening to our call."
Message from Archangel Michaël: April 29, 2015, 6:09 p.m.

§§§

Intuitive Prayer: April 4, 2015, Anne André

"Lord, it is so peaceful to be back in your fullness and your serenity
For here in this silence and contemplation of your glory and
your infinite love.
I have no voice and my eyes amazed by so much beauty, wonders
I don't even want to go back on earth to accomplish my
mission there.
I like this quiet state where I am when I find you
I draw energies from your divine light, your kindness, your
beauty, generosity and infinite love.

I piled them into my heart and in my soul to be able to share
the other down here
Do me the favor of all these beautiful things coming from you.
Give me your strength, your light, your gifts of healing,
Your compassionate glances and tenderness towards others
Also for those who like you and do not know you or do not
want to know you.
Purify me of being judgmental towards those ones and to
accept them as they are
And open my heart more and more to those who most need
of your light through me coz they will find it.
I am a craftsman, an instrument of your peace, your love,
your light
I love to travel up to you as I love this tranquility in me, this
state of infinite ecstasy.
On the rise to the next level where everything is more
beautiful, more love
My God shape me, model me in your image
So I could be a reflection of your own down here image.
From the little I have, so much I can do;
With you by my side, I have absolutely nothing to fear.
With you the impossible becomes possible; I believe ... yes
I believe
You were always there, even in the worst moments.
You never left me, you even brought me several times
I was tired to continue; I was completely exhausted.
You took me in your arms and you carried me and put me
back on my feet
And stronger you make me to cross the fields of thorns.
To finally get to the fields of flowers where everything is
so beautiful

And all colorful and with extraordinary scents.

Yes Lord, you helped me to go beyond what I have been able to go, with you I did it

With your help, with your angels, archangels, your guides, yes I arrived

And I am this day just to prove to you my gratitude by telling you a big thank you.

Thank you for being there every passing day and each night also.

I love you all you all beings of divine light

I love you, I love us. I feel so good in your presence.

You always give me inner peace and strength

To keep moving forward on my journey here on earth.

I have no fear, I will not fear as Lord you are here with and near me

And as long as you all light beings you are there

At my side to support me in my mission on this earth."

§§§

My next book will include all the inspirational writings from beyond the veil.

Original of Mum's messages in French through automatic/
spirit writings.

Spirit Writings: June 30, 2003; Start Time 5:30 p.m. End Time 5:40 p.m.

Me: Mum, what can we do to become better and to obtain God's blessings in each of our lives?

Mum: Love each other without limitation. Give a heart full of love to your worst enemies. Love, love, love –starting within your own family.

Me: Mum, it is so awesome to talk to you. How is this possible? Tell me.

Mum: I am full of emotion too. Fortunately, I have permission to use your hand and tell you that I am okay where I am. Everything is love and beauty. Tell the others not to cry over me. I am so happy where I am. There are many people that I loved and that I saw again. We all found each other. Tell Benji[6] that I am proud of him. I see each day how he took my place. Stay united always, and live love together always. I love you so much—your mum who feels your love too. I love you.

§§§

Strange the way Mum always focused on saying, "stay united". I am increasingly convinced that God itself is making this book available this year. It is my responsibility to write Mum's messages down, compile them into a book, publish it, and share it, with love, with all of you: beings of light. I do not know why she chose me for this. I can't change my past, my mistakes, my grudges, my misunderstandings,

---

[6]   Sibling Fictitious Name.

my anger, my truths, my frustrations, my doubts, my pains, or my big mouth. However, I can change my way of thinking and my actions right now. I may have done many bad things in my life that harmed many people, especially in the past, but I learned from my mistakes and grew a lot from them. I try each day to make a new start towards a new me, especially after my awakening.

For so long, I blamed myself for all my misdeeds, but I finally accepted my faults and let go. God had already forgiven me of everything, and he loves me more than anyone else could. I only had to feel remorse and repentance and keep myself from making the same mistake again. Yes, his love is much more than I could ever imagine. He never blamed me or judged me for anything. Therefore, I should thank him for his eternal love, compassion, and care towards me, a lost soul on this earth, trying to remember who I am and what I came here to experience. Every experience we go through has a purpose, as we need to experience both the good and the bad to know the difference. I may not be proud of the bad things I've done, but good things came out of it. I needed to experience it to move closer to the good. If I did not go through the events of the past several years, I would not be where I am or, more importantly, who I am. It is hard to remember that we may have already been in certain circumstances before, prompting déjà vu. However, we cannot control what we already experienced in past lives as an endless experience of who we are. We are one in all and all in one; we are all in God, and God is in us all. If we are all one, we are all the same; there is no separation of colour, race, religion, or belief. We are all connected, whether we like it or not. God is everything, and we are part of everything, so are we part of God itself; therefore, we are one with God. Moreover, the Lord loves each of us the same amount—endlessly. Therefore, what we see is an illusion, as everything is pure energy and pure love. We are not here to accumulate possessions, to build an empire, to buy houses for the next generation, or to work hard to accumulate wealth. No, we are here to learn only one thing: how to love everything and everyone without judgment. We are supposed to live love in the light of our life path and to experience love in all its beauty, majesty, and essence forever. Get rid of any ego and detach from any material vice, as we are here for our love for one another to grow.

By reading this book, you made the right decision to turn your life around. Always remember that God forgives any wrong things you have done. God the Father, Son, and Holy Spirit, all in one and one in all, are the epitome of non-judgmental, unconditional, and endless love. He is almighty, good, truth, and holy, and he loves you dearly. Do not feel ashamed of your bad actions; he will never judge you, as he gave you free will; he will not harm you for any wrong you have done. He loves you more than anyone else does, and he will open his arms to you, no matter what. God will never let you leave him, as his love is far beyond what humans can imagine. In light of how much he loves you, try not to make the same mistakes or commit the same sins again. In addition, remember that we need the good and the bad experiences to learn and grow. Therefore, there is no wrong! It's part of life experience. We need darkness in order to see the stars.

Inspirational Writing: March 18, 2014, Anne André

In life, sometimes we really have no other choice than to deal with a situation either the best [way] or worst way we can; that's okay. We did the best we possibly could at the time. Do not feel guilty; you are much loved, even when you feel so weak and so dirty inside and outside. We are human, with human feelings, but God is from paradise and is pure light and love. He loved, loves, and always will love us; and, especially when we fall down, he always gives us a hand to get up on our feet and clean ourselves, and he wipes our sins white as snow and looks to the future, for what's best for us. Moreover, if we are too weak to make a further step, he even carries us for a while until we get better. God bless you all who accept and forgive yourselves for your weaknesses. Forgive yourselves, and look ahead what you can do better and be better.

§§§

Therefore, if others are judging you, remember that God does not hate you, and he never will. Do not judge, and you will never be judged; do not stop loving yourself, as God will never stop loving you. Trust God, as he will always be present for you and lend you a hand in the most difficult times, lift you up, and put you back on your feet. He will give you new opportunities to become better. Therefore, ask him for his help, and he will be there. Call upon him and see that he is near you, listening to your prayers always. Never give up, dear ones. Trust and pray for better days and a better life. Ask for his angels' assistance. They are waiting for your call. They will not impose themselves upon you, but if you ask them for help, they are happy to help instantly in every sense of the word. They are there to protect you and guide you in the right direction, so don't hesitate to call upon angels, archangels, spirit guides, higher masters, saints, and God if you feel the motivation. Follow your heart and turn your thoughts to them, and they will be immediately near you, ready to help and guide you.

We all face challenges; for example, some people may have lost a child or several children; some may have lost their parents young and experienced adoption; and some may have had fertility issues and never had a child of their own after several attempts or in vitro methods. Some people are born with a disability or care for a child with a disability; some people are homeless; and some feel hopeless and lost in life. People may be gay, lesbian, bisexual, or transsexual; some people have AIDS; other people may have no food to eat, no water to drink, or no clothes to wear; some have to spend their lifetimes in prison or suffer a long stay in a hospital. Some people have had an abortion; others may have an incurable disease, cancer, leukaemia, or loss of sight or hearing; some people must be in a wheelchair; others have experienced sexual abuse or rape. Some people have multiple personalities; some people face depression and require a psychologist or psychiatrist throughout their lifetimes. Thus, we each have challenges to overcome. It is not an easy path, but we have help from above to help us in our journey. We don't remember it, but maybe we asked for our particular life; remember that we have several previous lives, and we came back to experience the completeness of our soul. Therefore, maybe we asked to experience the sadness of losing a child or to deal with growing up on our own. Maybe we asked to be homeless, with nothing to rely on but ourselves and the love and charity of others. Perhaps we asked to be sick or to experience AIDS or cancer. Who knows? The memory may be in our minds, but we cannot remember it if we do not elevate ourselves to awaken our third eye, go deeper, and connect our spiritual mind to our soul. Otherwise, we will just live our life here and leave it without doing anything new or remembering the purpose for which we came back.

Life is a journey for remembering what we failed to do in our past lives; each time we come back, we stay stagnant or make progress. To do the latter, we see beyond what people normally see, hear beyond what they normally hear, and feel beyond what they normally feel. We are a step higher than others are. If we can see the beauty in nature, we can communicate more easily with everything in heaven. Watch a flower; see its colour and its scent; isn't it as beautiful as God is? Look at the beauty of nature—the ocean, a river, a cascade, a valley, a mountain, the snow, the sun, the stars, the sky, the rain, and the rainbow. Aren't these things beautiful to the eye, and aren't they God himself? Feel the breeze on your face; hear the birds singing; feel the peace under a tree; watch the shape of the clouds and the waves crashing on the beach. Isn't this amazing to experience? You get to be part of all this, to become one with these things which are God, meaning you are God yourself when you are in communion with everything and everyone that is God. There are infinite possibilities, and as we are made in God's image, aren't we each beautiful in a unique way? Moreover, remember that God is everything, and everything is God. Nothing is separate from God. We are able to feel, to give, and to receive love as God; we are love in all its divinity. Yes, we are all divine, in fact.

Chapter 5

WE ARE ALL PSYCHICS

Spirit Writings: July 1, 2003; Start Time 11:10 a.m. End Time 12:15 p.m.

Me: Mum, it is I. I know you are still with all the others and me. I would like to ask on Antoine's[7] behalf: who are the people that you know so well and that are with you in heaven? I'm waiting for your response. Please take my hand and write what only you can tell me.

Mum: Good morning. I hope you told everyone about my messages, as it is important that you all know the chance that we have to be in contact with each other. There are so many people around me, friends I had lost years ago, whom I found again and whom I esteemed a lot. Arlette,[8] Sylvain,[9] and Dominic,[10] are beautiful angels who surround Mary, the blessed

---

[7]   Sibling Fictitious Name.

[8]   My sister passed on at the age of two.

[9]   My brother passed on at only four months old.

[10]   My nephew passed on at two weeks.

mother. She is the one who intercedes for us and blesses us for our good actions. There are also three other angels from our family; they never made it on earth. They are much more beautiful, and they help us to look more beautiful. Much goodness falls upon us and on you because of their missions. Their intervention pushes aside much danger. I have met many friends and members of the family here.[11]

We were surprised to find out that Mum met people we did not think would be in heaven.

This is another reason my family grew more doubtful about the source of the messages, as they could not believe that a given person was in heaven and others were in purgatory or hell. To date, debates are still going on, and some members of the family don't approve of what Mum said. For them, it was simply impossible that this could be the case. They considered it all blasphemy. I felt bad after communicating with Mum on this subject, as I did not want to hurt anyone's feelings concerning these revelations. I had the duty of sharing the information, but certain family members told me to watch what I said. That's why I am not publicly using the names that were given to me. However, if any member of my family has any questions on this, I am more than willing to share any of these given information personally to them.

§§§

---

[11]   Many names of family members cited, but for privacy reasons, I can't name them publicly here.

Spirit Writings: July 2, 2013; Start Time 8:30 a.m. End Time 9:22 a.m.

Me: Good Morning, Mum. Lydia[12] thanks you for talking about Dominic. Do you have a message for her? When you are ready, Mum, let me know.

Mum: I am happy for her. Many lost souls were found and saved when Dominic passed over. Lydia's strong belief places her continuously under divine protection, and God loves her so much. We all love her. Her prayers protect the whole family from bad things. Tell her to strengthen her belief. She will be rewarded for this. The Virgin Mary walks by her side. Lydia has a charitable and saintly education. She knows how to convey it to her family and others. Tell her to continue in her faith always. Tell her thanks for her goodness towards others and me. If she knew how her son and my children[13] are beautiful and how they work for God, she would be so happy. She would bless the day they passed over. Tell her that I love her and her saintly family.

Me: Thank you, Mum, for that wonderful message. Mum, please reassure me that you are the one writing, and it is not my imagination.

Mum: Yes, Noël,[14] I am the one writing to you. You shouldn't have any doubt. I am with you always.

§§§

---

[12] Sister Fictitious name (Dominic's mum)
[13] Arlette and Sylvain, my sister and brother in heaven
[14] Abbreviated middle name—also means Christmas.

I was so happy that mum confirmed that she was speaking to me and it was not my imagination. The communication became easier and clearer, and I was overwhelmed with joy. You too can do it—everyone can. If you are not scared of your loved ones talking to you from the other side, I encourage you to engage in such communication. However, make sure that your loved ones are really the entity with you, as anyone can be talking to you. When you open the door to other dimensions, anyone can get in, including low spirits in the dark realm. Therefore, always ask for angelic protection, particularly Archangel Michael. Say, "Archangel Michael, please protect me from all dark forces, negative spirits, and negative thoughts. I only want to communicate with my loved ones who are with the angels and archangels and the spirit and master guides in the white light. Only allow the spirits of love near me. I thank you. I ask this through Jesus Christ. Amen." After that, try the following method: Close your eyes, think deeply of your loved ones, and call upon them. Clear your mind of any thoughts or distractions like bills you have to pay, what's on the TV, what you are going to cook for dinner, what you are going to wear the next day, and so forth. Breathe in and out. Light a candle in a quiet room, with a dim light, or place a photo of your loved one in front of you with some flowers and a glass of water nearby. Go into deep meditation, thinking about your loved one. You can try the method I used, with a blank piece of paper and a pen ready for use. Alternatively, you can type what comes to mind as answers; your loved ones can talk to you through your thoughts. Just type the first thoughts that come into your mind, without thinking about anything else. On the other hand, if you are using paper and pen, let your loved ones take control of your hands, and your loved ones will guide you to write what they want to communicate with you. You will be surprised to see what answers you receive. Listen to your instincts and your heart, and ask your guardian angel for guidance. You can even ask your spirit guides to help make the communication possible between you and your loved ones.

Everything is possible where love exists. Therefore, if a strong bond existed between you and your loved ones who passed on to the spirit world, the love continues. It is no longer a physical love for that person, but a spiritual one. They are still the person who they were before, but they are now spirits of love—sources of infinite love. However, you can still see, feel, and hear them. When you close your eyes, call upon them, and listen to what they have to tell or show you through your thoughts, they are ready to guide you. They will not interfere in your decisions or your life, as you have free will. However, they will be there to help if you ask. Some of these entities could be your spiritual guides, and they help you find answers to your questions. Yes, you can do it, as we are all born psychics!

Chapter 6

THE DEAD ARE ALIVE, WELL, AND NEARBY

Spirit Writings: July 1, 2003; Start Time 7:15 p.m. End Time 8:30 p.m.

Me: Mum, it's a joy for me to meet you again finally. I want you to tell me what is wrong with Robert.[15] Why does he seem so depressed and unsuccessful in anything he undertakes? I await your answer Mum.

Mum: **Poor man. Tell him that I did not give up on him and that I still love him. I am hurt when he suffers. I know that he always cries to me. There is a lot of jealousy surrounding him and in his family. Tell him to continue having faith; he is on the right track. Tell him also to purify his heart and to forgive even his enemies. His heart will then be free of any resentment that is harming himself and his group. Tell him to persevere in his faith and his prayers and to get rid of all the jealousy. I want him to know**

---

[15] Fictitious name of a member of our family

that I will protect him still. My loved one, do not be sad to have lost me. I am now able to help you more from where I am. You will see life change for you shortly. However, I see that your family is badly in need of your support more than ever. You will have a difficult ordeal to suffer soon, but know that faith and prayer will protect you and your family. You will not have to fear anything. My dear, I will always be close to you and your family. You are all under my protection; my love for you is great, children of my heart. I love you all. Do not give up your daily prayer. God waits for it every moment.

§§§

Spirit Writings: July 3, 2003; Start Time 11:00 a.m. End Time 11:30 a.m.

Me: Hello, Mum. It's I—Noël. Are you still with me?
Mum: Hello, Noël. I am always with you.
Me: Would you tell me something special—something only for me?
Mum: Watch that the family remains united, and make an effort for harmony to reign at home. Fill your home with love where there is indifference. Love each member of your family more than you currently do. Love, love, love always in your everyday life. Take care of yourself, my dear Noël. Your mum loves you deeply and says thank you again that you were there whenever I had need of you. I kiss you. I am near you every second and always will be. Mum loves you

so much. **Kiss Caroline[16] and Loïc[17] for me; tell the children that Dada[18] constantly watches over them. I love them all.**

§§§

Spirit Writings: July 3, 2003; Start Time 7:30 p.m. End Time 8:30 p.m.

Me: Mum, I wanted to tell you again that we all love you and always will. You are with me — with us all—every moment. None of your children will ever forget you. Do you have a message for us?

Mum: I would like all of you to remember my eternal love. Always live in harmony with each other. Stay united. You are all so dear to my heart. I love you more than ever. I am happy where I am. I never saw such beautiful things on earth. I wish to welcome you when the time comes for you to be with me. It is wonderful and infinitely beautiful here. We who exist here are beautiful, and when we step forwards, we become more beautiful. The more we love, the more we become beautiful. You too should share love around you and be humble in your actions towards others. To be with God our Holy Father, who loves you unconditionally and endlessly, love always. Be good to each other, and be true in your actions and thoughts. God hears every prayer, so tell

---

[16] My daughter
[17] My son
[18] Mum's nickname, as she didn't like being called "grandma"

him everything. He will guide you each day of your life. Do not forget our mother, queen of heaven and earth, and mother of Jesus, the immaculate Virgin Mary. She intercedes continuously for you and for us before God, our immense light. I love you. I am still alive; I will always be near you and will protect you all always.

§§§

I felt sad when she again insisted we remain united. This did not happen at all, unfortunately. I am my mother's voice, and I know that she never wanted this. If she were still here with us, this would never have happened. However, I know that she also knows how it turned out, and she wants us to move on and live our life. She told us this through a reading with a recognized medium. Maybe her sadness will make some of us realize that we all came from the same mother and that we should hold on to each other. May God help us all realize that we should live in peace and love with each other, now and forever.

Don't hold grudges against other members of your family. Live in harmony and peace always, as your loved ones want you to live in the light, love, and truth. If you are not talking to a member of your family, make a phone call, say hello, ask how he or she is doing, and offer your love. You will feel much better after doing this. This will fill your heart with relief, love, and happiness. You have freed yourself of grudges, hate, misunderstandings, envy, and all negative feelings, and you will feel good about yourself. You will feel an abundance of love that you have never experienced before. Do it now, as you may not have the chance to say or do anything tomorrow. You can make that special effort now in the name of love. We can all make this world a better place. If each one of us experiences forgiveness in our hearts, we will also experience peace and love, and when we experience such positive feelings, we are able to share this abundance with others. So, go make that phone call or visit now; it will make a big difference. Moreover, if the person still ignores and resents you afterwards, then forgive him or her and move on with your life; know that you did your best for now.

Looking back, I realize that I'm still trying to forgive others and myself. However, in the end, do we need to forgive or ask for forgiveness when our hearts are full of pure love and empty of resentment? I do not think that we have to mention the word. In fact, there is no need for a cycle of forgiveness if we release the hate in our heart. When we meet again one day, we will give each other a beautiful smile and a warm hug as if nothing bad ever happened. It will be all about love. Forgiveness and love are in your eyes and your gestures—a kind hug or a gentle smile. Therefore, make peace with each other and enjoy each other's company now, no matter when you expect to see your loved ones again in this physical world.

I have sacrificed a lot to get where I am today. I have worked seven days a week, doing three different jobs—more than seventy hours a week—for more than five continuous years to make a living as a single mum with two children. Most of my siblings despised me when I expressed my feelings to them. I have experienced homelessness, financial crisis, stress, depression, anxiety, illnesses, and hunger, but now I am grateful for my blessings. I am proud that I never gave up on life amidst all its challenges.

From now on, I will practice love, light, care and truth. I believe that Jesus, God, or whichever deity or higher power in which you believe is not judging you for anything. I do not follow any specific religion; to me, all religions bring us to God. I do not believe in a God who punishes us for our sins or discriminates against those who did something bad. I do not believe he rejects those who are divorced or blame those who had abortions or committed suicide. I could not believe that God would be angry with us for doing such actions or living gay or lesbian lifestyles. On the contrary, I believe that he would be sad when anyone sins, and he would want us to live in his light. God is love, which means he can heal and forgive everything. Love instantly washes away guilt. For example, if you got pregnant after someone raped you when you were only ten years old, would you live with such guilt and have a child from such an awful experience? If you choose to have the baby, you are a brave person. However, if you chose not to have the baby, do you think God will hate you and punish you in addition to such a painful experience? No, dear ones, he would not. As long as you know that it wasn't good to do so but you didn't have a choice at the time, and if you feel deeply sorry for that terrible action, you are forgiven. There are so many beings of light, like angels, who are there to help you connect yourself to the source of light and to feel the love of the source, or God. This love will cleanse you and remove your fear and guilt. God is love, and he loves you so much. He is not a God that condemns; if you sin, he will tell you to go repent and do better. He gives you new chances every time you ask, because he is pure love and light.

As long as you feel sorry deep inside, repent and know that what you did might have hurt other souls, dear ones, the Lord forgives you. I stopped practicing any religion for a while, but that doesn't mean I have no faith. I follow my intuition and the things my heart feels. Love is priceless, so I will practice it until I leave this earth and beyond. Therefore, love is my religion and my only reality.

§§§

Spirit Writings: July 3, 2013; Start Time 9:05 p.m. End Time 9:40 p.m.

Me: Mum, would you have a message for Isabella?[19]

No answer.

Me: Mum, are you still here?
Mum: Yes, I am always here, Noël, my adorable child. Tell Isabella that my mother's love for her is more than eternal. Tell her to focus on her family life now. She was so worried for me. She does not have to worry anymore, as I have gotten rewards. I am happy in my new life. Tell her not to be discouraged. She can offer me all her sorrows, and I will give them rest. She has me in whom to confide. We must reject all bad thoughts and any reason for their existence. Tell her to give me all her moments of sadness, and

---

[19]   Fictitious name Sibling

I will transform them into moments of joy. I am closer to you than ever before. Let me help you in your suffering. I will give you rest. Have no fear. I am continuously at your side to take you where I want to take you. You will understand the purpose of my posts in time.

I want you to find this divine faith; it must have a vital role in your life. Dear one, turn towards prayer; it will be of great help—believe me. I'll help you as much as I can to regain confidence. I love you and will love you forever, your mum who loves you with an infinite love, —Gerda.

§§§

For the first time, Mum signed her name. When Mum signed her name, I had no doubt that it was really her writing and talking to me continuously. I was happy, and I shared this wonderful message with everyone in the family. My family members persisted in their doubt, but I would not give up. Mum was in my heart and mind more than ever, and I had a strong communication with her. I was channelling her. I attuned with her frequency, and I did not want to let go of that gift of hearing her guidance. She was like my spiritual guide, and I was honoured and grateful that this happened to me, as I loved Mum so much. My siblings loved her very much too, but I felt so happy to be able to share and receive these amazing messages from her.

One of our relatives was going through a tough time in her marriage, and she faced severe depression. On top of that, she deeply wanted to have a child but could not. Mum predicted that this relative would be a mum, despite several losses through the years. I understand today why Mum said what she said back then, as this relative was overseas back then, and her life has completely turned around. Today, she lives in a new country. She remarried and has two beautiful children, and she lives a happy life with her new husband and family in a brand new beautiful house. Everything turned out for the better for her. Heaven blessed her.

§§§

Spirit Writings: July 5, 2013; Start Time 11:50 a.m. End Time 1:05 p.m.

Me: Mum, I am so emotional, writing you these few words. I would like to remind you of my eternal love and to thank you for all your beautiful messages of love. Marilyn[20] and Sylvio[21] are the only ones for whom I have not yet requested a few words. Would you share something special to say to each of them? I'm expecting you, lovely mum—Noëlette, who thinks of you all the time and carries you always in her heart.

Mum: My Noël, deeply loved: I'm emotional too that you would address me after this long silence. I know that you still have doubts about my existence. You buried my body, but my spirit is still alive. I am continually near you to help you change your lives and get closer to the holy deity.[22] We do not ask you to change but to contribute as much love as you can. You started to understand, because I see you making

---

[20]   Fictitious name Sibling

[21]   Fictitious name Sibling

[22]   Divinity

great efforts in your home. If you continue, you will see love bring you everything that you might expect. Hi, my dear Marilyn. I am glad you send this little message. You have suffered a lot in your poor life. Know that your sufferings will allow you to get many blessings. Do not think that God sent you those problems by pure coincidence; no, there is a goal behind them. Never doubt his immense love for you. Keep faith in him, and you will experience rewards. Do not be sad that you do not see me anymore. Console yourself by knowing that I see you all. I will always be by your side to guide you. Carry love in your heart always for all those who surround you. Practice charity always—learn how to be a charitable being and humble in your heart. Open your eyes to see hands in need of help and to hear the calls of the deaf. You have the power to contribute to a better land. May peace reign in your family always. Keep your faith intact, despite the trials and struggles.

Leave me your distress, and I will give you rest from all your headaches and your moments of discouragement that prevent you from seeing clearly most of the time. I love you and will protect you and the members of your family always.

My dear Sylvio, forgive me if I sometimes did wrong by you. I know that God has already forgiven all my mistakes, so do not have any resentment for me in your heart either. Think of the wonderful moments we had together.

I know that right now, you are hopeless about life. Do not be like this. Continue to confide in the Lord, as he knows your pain and sorrow. There is a time for everything, and these are tests to see how you will respond. Do not drop your arms now. Moments of happiness are waiting for you and your son. I cannot tell you more, but you must remain confident. God never abandons one of his children. Spread love and have understanding and tolerance towards others. Aid those who ask for it without hesitation. God will repay you someday. Take good care of your little one. God will be grateful for that, and you will see the blessings he sends to you both. I love you with an exceptional love. I will always be here for you. From Mum, who will love you always.

Me: Thanks, Mum. I will not forsake you; believe me.

§§§

Spirit Writings: July 5, 2013; Start 10:00 p.m. End Time 10:30 p.m.

Me: Mum, are you here with us? I am home with Susan[23] and Thomas.[24] Do you have something special to tell us? I'm waiting for you, Mum.

Mum: Yes, Noël, I am with you and always will be. I am happy to see you all together at home. If only you knew the joy that you bring me. Live always like this, in harmony with each other. I see you. You are all so dear to my humble heart. Wherever love is, God is among you. I will always be near you. Mum

---

[23]   Sister Fictitious name
[24]   Brother Fictitious name

will always love you and guide you each day. Have no fear. I will act upon your thoughts, and you will see the results soon. I love you.—Gerda

Me: Thanks, Mum. We love you so much. Be happy, Mum.

§§§

As I went back through all these memories, tears fell from my eyes to my chin. I felt Mum's presence so intensely, and I felt her hand on mine in a way that affected me deeply. There was no doubt in my mind that it was her. I was experiencing something out of the ordinary, beyond imagination. I felt her presence behind me and over me. You would call me a clairsentient and clairaudient medium. However, I was not aware at that time that I could have psychic abilities or act as a medium. For those who have never experienced this, I hope that you will very soon. You can tell me about the wonderful feelings you experienced, how happy you felt, and how tremendously love embraced your heart at that moment. In addition, you will know that nothing separates you from anyone, especially from your loved ones in the spirit world. They are closer to you than you would imagine. Every moment, they hear you and are near you. Never forget that.

Do not say, "Leave the dead with the dead". You have it all wrong, Rather, treat the dead as alive, and they will be present in your life until you meet again back home. They always want you to remember them and to ask them for help and guidance. Moreover, they want you think of them, and they will be near you to help and guide you, now and always. They are always waiting for your call. Be more receptive to them and their messages, and you will know how alive they remain.

Chapter 7

DUTIES ON THE OTHER SIDE

Spirit Writings: July 8, 2013; Start Time 5:35 p.m. End Time 5:50 p.m.

Me: Mum, it's I—Noël: your daughter who loves you. I put on your favourite waltz. Do you hear it?

Mum: Yes, what a beautiful melody, Noël. What a beautiful idea you had. All the angels here are dancing around me. It is magical. Immense happiness surrounds us. You made me experience such a beautiful moment. Thank you, Noël, child of my humble heart, for this beautiful and wonderful gift. It makes me so happy, and it makes me realize the important place I hold in your heart. Everything is more beautiful around me with this music playing. Thank you again, Noël, for thinking of this surprise. I am deeply touched. I kiss you and hold you close to my heart. I hear my favourite waltz, Noëlette. How delightful! Kiss everyone for me: the children, grandchildren, and great-grandchildren. I want no one to doubt anymore the deep love I have for you all.

§§§

When I first contacted my mum this way, it was to get something on paper. Making contact was hard, and it was so hard to understand what I had written. With more frequent contact, it was much easier to obtain the information and much easier to decode the messages. Now that I have opened the door, I am accepting these messages and believing in them. Some family members were not supportive, as mentioned previously. They told me that I should not disturb the dead, especially our dead mum. They said that I should let her rest in peace. I felt lost at times, and I really did not know whether to go on or to stop, but my instincts told me that I should continue, so I did.

§§§

Spirit Writings: July 10, 2003; Start Time 6:00 p.m. End Time 6:40 p.m.

Me: Hi, dear Mum. I hope you have been overjoyed listening to your favourite songs that I put on for you. I would like to remind you of my eternal love for you, my adorable mum, as well as for Jesus Christ, the Virgin Mother Mary, the Lord, the angels, the saints, and all those who pray for us continuously in heaven or in paradise. Their prayers make us turn to the light and contribute to our improvement and development. Tell sister Arlette, brother Sylvain, and nephew Dominic as well as the other three little angels you were talking about that I'm proud of them, and I hold them close to my heart. I kiss you lovingly and hold you close to my heart. I love you forever. All your children send their eternal love and think very strongly of you. We are all proud of this day. If you want to tell me something, I am at your service, my dear mother. All the grandchildren send you their love. Thank you for making such an effort so that we realize the immense and eternal love of the Father, Son, and Holy Spirit. We promise, Mum, to improve, because we all want to find you again one day. We hope your breathtaking maternal love as well as the love of the Lord, the one and only God, will embrace us again. Be happy where you are, Mum. We are all happy that you reached the house of the Lord.

Mum: My dear and humble-of-heart Noëlette, how well you spoke. We bless you, and I know that your path will not end here, as you have many good actions to accomplish. Do not hesitate to change your life, as I have opened the door for you. Follow the road that brings you to love. Never stop praying each morning and night, and be grateful to God for all the joys and sorrows he brings you. I am here for a reason: to help you and enlighten you. Each day, I work in God's favour. Thank you, dear Noël, for playing my favourite songs. You touch my humble heart. My road to God was long, but I felt so much love when I reached him. You will see for yourself one day the endless love that embraces you when your time comes. Even though I was scared, I was going to God, so I also felt peace as I surrendered my soul to him completely. You too will abandon yourself to him, even though you've never seen him; he will embrace you with so much goodness.

§§§

Spirit Writings: July 18, 2003; Start Time 11:10 a.m. End
Time 11:40 a.m.

*Me: Mum, if you are near me, I would like to ask you about
Frank,[25] who is sad presently. Would you have some words
of comforts for him? He goes back home soon as you must
know. I wait patiently to hear your message whenever you
want, Mum.*

**Mum: Noël, it has been a long time, and I have
been waiting for this moment. Never doubt the
truthfulness of my messages. God allowed us to have
this contact, so do not abandon me. My messages
are ways for me to be near you and guide you on
the right path. Don't ever dare to doubt that I
cannot help you improve your life. Tell Frank not
to cry for me anymore. I am well and happy. Tell
him to face his future with his family. I was selfish
for wanting to keep him to myself. God reminded
me that a man has to leave his father and mother
and be with his wife to form a family. I kept him
all that time and almost forgot how much his wife
and children needed him. Tell him that his decision
makes me enormously happy. From now on, he must
turn to, look after, and testify his love to his wife
and children. Tell him not to be sad like this; when
grief enters the soul, it is very difficult to get out. I
will always be beside him, as he was next to me until
the last moments. I will help as much as I can. Tell**

---

[25] Fictitious name of a member of our family

him that discouragement will not bring anything positive for him and his family, because it gives evil the opportunity to serve its purpose. Tell him not to be worried; everything has a solution. I know all about his hidden problems. Tell him to continue to pray and to strengthen his faith in the Holy Spirit. He will see the light at the end of the tunnel. Tell him to pray for others as well. God loves it when one does not think only of him- or herself. Tell Frank that I will be by his side every moment and that for any decision he has to make, I will act on his thoughts for him to take the good path. He only has to confide in me, and I will refresh him from all his troubles. Tell him that nothing is lost and that we shall meet again one day, because I am still alive and well. For now, change your lives on earth and improve your soul, for God will take account of this. Noël,[26] kiss all the children for me. Tell them I love them all, and be happy for me.

My dear one, I give you back to your family. You freed me, and I became more beautiful and happier. Go find your little family, and fight and live for them from now on. Do not ever forget about your family. I love you dearly. I embrace you all.

—Mum

Mum warned me, as she knew I had doubts in my head and in my heart, as I was listening to what the others told me and not to what my instincts and intuition said. Mum was always right, as she did what she promised and looked

---

[26] Nickname of mine

after this particular member of the family; this person is doing very well today. He immigrated with his family, and they live happily in their new country, in a brand new home. Everything has changed for the better.

§§§

Spirit Writings: July 24, 2003; Start Time 1:35 p.m. End Time 4:10 p.m.

Me: Mum, it's I—Noël. If you are nearby, talk to me. I need to hear your words of comfort and love. Forgive me for not writing to you earlier. Sometimes I am too emotional to let you hold my hand and write what you want to tell me. I love you, Mum. I went home. It seemed so empty without you there. You and dad left emptiness in our lives, and it is sometimes hard to accept this reality. However, our faith is growing with your help, Mum. On behalf of all your children, I would like to tell you that we love you.

Mum: Noël, don't be so sad. I am near you. When you are sad, so am I. I know how difficult it is to admit that I am gone, but have faith that I never abandoned you all and never will. Keep your faith in our Father, his Son, and the Holy Spirit, and live your life in accordance with the divine words and righteousness. Never lose faith. Remain strong, as Satan watches for your weaknesses. I will always be nearby to protect you. I know you are suffering inside because you are telling yourself that it happened quickly. I know your thoughts, and I know you feel sad and discouraged. You seem like a lost sheep, but God looks after his sheep. He will not let your lives go

on like this forever. Everything has a purpose. Noël, now that you know how many changes are going to happen in your lives, you will see improvements in time; you will understand that I passed over for a reason. Be strong, Noël, and be courageous. I am here. Don't fear anything. I will never abandon you or the others. I am your mum, who loves you.

§§§

Spirit Writings: July 30, 2003; Start Time 11:00 a.m. End Time 11:40 a.m.

Me: Mum, it's I—Noël. Do you have a message for the others and me? I'm waiting, Mum."

Mum: "Noël, my child, I wait for this moment with such impatience, as I come to you with immense pleasure. My life here is very busy, as I have things to do that I accomplish with astonishment. These little jobs are quite different from those I was doing on earth. I am much more resourceful here, and I help many people in despair. I help them find courage again. I am by their side in their moments of sorrow, and I help them have faith again. I also help them pray to God, our creator, his son, Jesus, who gave his life for our sins, the Holy Spirit, who gives us life and light, and Mary, queen of heaven. Noël, I am so happy to see the change in your lives and attitudes. Continue this way, all of you. Look for the essential in your lives. Seeking God in each of us is a priority, as he is love. He is present in each person, no matter what his or her race or social standing is. That is why you

should not criticize rich people or tread on the poor ones. God made us all in his image. Noël, I do not regret my life on earth or its end. Everything is much better here; you may think I am selfish saying this, but one day you will understand why I would not want to return to my sad life on earth. Everything here is peace and love. There are many wonderful people, and I am very busy doing good works.

Me: Thanks, Mum, for your message. One last little thing: Rosemary[27] tried the automatic/spirit writings and got a small message from you. However, she thinks that they were her thoughts. If it is true, could you confirm to Rosemary and me that you would like to be in contact with her?

Mum: Yes, I tried to be in contact with Rosemary, but she should not doubt. Otherwise, it will not work. She is happy, and she knows how to pray to God. She must continue in her Christian faith, and she will experience rewards on earth and afterward. Her descendants shall benefit from her great goodness to others. She is good and does not hesitate to help others. I kiss her strongly and thank her for all her prayers for others.

§§§

It seems as if life was going on normally for Mum, as she was working and liked what she was doing. Friends and family members all worked in harmony to help us, guide us, and influence us. Sometimes my inner voice might be from

---

27   Related

her. She seemed happy, and she seemed to love her new life. That was the only thing that mattered to me. I wonder if they have a home, a garden, or a life like the ones they had on earth. If someone was a florist, maybe he or she was still doing the same job there; if someone loved to work with children, maybe he or she is in charge of the little ones who have passed on, helping them grow in heaven. If someone was a famous singer on earth, maybe he or she sings for God and directs a fabulous choir, with all the angels, singing for the glory of God in a wonderful concert. If someone was a great painter on earth, maybe that person makes beautiful paintings in heaven. Who knows what that life is like? However, I believe that it would be amazing, full of care for each other, awareness of God's love for each of us, love for each other, and cooperation in working together. How amazing it would be to be on this wonderful team, working in the name of Jesus Christ, his Father, and the Holy Spirit. The varieties and bright colours of the light and flowers would be amazing. There are infinite possibilities of existence and awareness. How beautiful heaven might be. You might be able to touch something and change it into another thing, or maybe you could be in several places at the same time.

Chapter 8

DOUBTS AND TRANSFORMATION

Spirit Writings: August 8, 2003; Start Time 3:00 am End Time 3:40 am

Me: Mum, I write to you again with great emotion, as sometimes I don't know whether I am disturbing you in your new life. Perhaps I have to let you live it, knowing that you are happy, and live mine here on earth. All of us still suffer from your absence. Francesca[28] sends you her love and holds you close in her arms. We all love you still, Mum. I will not forget you, even if I decide not to be in contact with you anymore. You will always remain in my heart and in your other children's hearts, wherever you are. Your messages have been of so much comfort, and what you sent will guide us each day. We promise to change for the better and to follow all your words. Would you like us to continue contacting you? Tell me what you want me to do. Alternatively, work on our thoughts, and show me the way

---

[28]   Family member

to go. *Am I taking the right direction? Mum, please tell me
what is right to do.*

*I do not want you to feel that I am abandoning you because I
am not writing to you anymore. For me, it is such a comfort
to read your words and let you guide me. Do you think it
is right to continue to write to each other? I am so afraid
of going the wrong way. Please reassure me and guide me.*

**Mum: My dear daughter, I love you and my other
children so much. The changes that are taking place
in you are enjoyable to watch from here. Continue to
follow the path on which I am guiding you, as you
are all under my protection. It is out of the question
that any of you will get lost.**

**Do you wonder why you no longer feel like yourself?
I am present to give you light, to guide you, and to
open your eyes to everything that you would not see
before. When I passed over, you became conscious
of so many things. Pray, my children, and let the
prayers become part of your daily life. God waits
each second for an act or a word from you. Do not
forget that he is everywhere, especially where you
would not think he is. Dear children, always have
faith and believe in him. He will never abandon you.
Noël, I understand your negative feelings concerning
our contact. Do you think that I would do this against
God's will? Never! God allows this communication
as a way of accomplishing part of my missions. You
are free to write to me whenever you feel the desire
or wish to do so. I will always be here when you ask
for me. You have nothing to fear, Noël. Don't you
see how I act upon your thoughts? I am bringing**

**you where you need to go, and I see that you follow
me with closed eyes, as you trust me. Let the Holy
Spirit guide you, Noël, and do not give up. You do
not have to worry about the writings if you do not
want to pursue them. However, I will always answer
if you feel you need to keep doing them. I will act
on your thoughts more, and you will tell me about
them.**

**Tell the others that I will act on their thoughts too,
and they will feel my presence nearby. They will
remember what I wish to happen, a complete change
in your life, bringing you all closer to God.**

Mum loves you all.

After this message, as I was becoming more and more
sceptical and felt increasing pressure from the family to
stop these communications. On the recommendation of my
sister Monique, I brought all the messages to a priest in my
parish, who told me that he would read them and talk to the
bishop about it. He told me that the love between my mum
and me was so powerful that it made this happen. He said
that our mum loved us so much that she was interceding
with the Holy Spirit to bring good changes in our lives and
not to doubt anymore that my mum was still alive in the
spirit world. He told me that he would get back to me soon.
I was relieved when I heard what he said as I thought he
would say that I was completely crazy. Another father from
the same parish knew about the manuscript, and he helped
me in my spiritual development and guided me through a
very difficult time in my life.

§§§

Spirit Writings: August 15, 2013; Start Time 12:55 p.m. End Time 01:10 p.m.

Me: Mum, I am at your place, and it is the feast of the Assumption.[29] Do you have a message for us, your children? Please kiss Mother Mary for me, and tell her that I love her dearly.

Mum: My dearest children, have a beautiful feast of the Assumption. May peace be among you and joy overflow your heart. Here, everything is amazing, and Mary is so beautiful on this joyful day. I would like you all to see this. Really, heaven is amazing and beautiful, and everything shines all around us. I kiss you all, your mum, who loves you. Have a wonderful and memorable day. Mary sends you her eternal love and blessing.

§§§

The days went by, and I would not give up on her. Even though the messages were distant, I believed that I had to continue. I had to have some evidence that these writings were true, and one day I would be able to prove they came from the spirit world, where my mum's new home was. Therefore, I took up my pen again nearly three weeks later.

Spirit Writings: September 8, 2013; Start Time 11:10 p.m. End Time 12:00 p.m.

---

[29] A day when Catholics—remember the ascension of the Virgin Mary into heaven

Me: Mum, are you always near me? Do you have a message for us today? Would you please tell us something from where you are? You are always in our thoughts, Mum, and we let ourselves guided by you, a being of light. Blessed are you, Mama, on this day and forever. Please kiss Mother Mary for me, because on this day, the church celebrates her proudly. She the Blessed Mother of God, who carried the saviour of humanity in her womb. I love you, Mum. Memories haunt us, but we keep hope that someday we will meet you again in the joy and the kingdom of God and our saviour.

Mum: **My dear Noël, my heart overflows with joy at this renewing of our contact. Your words touched my heart, as I know that God is in the centre of your life. Never give up, Noël. Light and joy are at the end of the road. Pray, my children, as you will find comfort and peace. Do not give up going to mass. Take communion; this is the way that the Holy Spirit will be within you, and you will become much stronger and be able to thwart evil.**

Do not be sad when you think about me. I am alive. You cannot see me, but whenever one of you thinks of me, I will be near you. This call from your heart is a love connection between you and me that I cannot dismiss without answering.

Console each other, children of my humble heart. Be saints, and act righteously towards each other. Do not forget that Jesus, God, and the Holy Spirit are in each of you.

I will always be closer to you than you could imagine. Carefully listen to me in your inner self, as it is there

that I am calling. Be aware of the wonderful things around you. Do not waste your time on useless things of no importance.

Find love through others, and share love always. It is the greatest gift that you could give to someone.

Mum is leaving you now and will come back soon. Do not forget—call me in your heart, and I will run to you. The God of Light and the Virgin Mary, our Holy Mother, give you their blessing.

I love you all infinitely.

—Gerda, your mum

§§§

Since Mum passed over, I needed support and did not know where to find it anywhere other than the church, so I attended daily mass at 6:30 a.m. I did not miss one day. I was getting closer and closer to the spiritual world, and it was magical. I felt Mum near me all the time. Everything around me had changed, and I was changing into a better me. Yes it was a NEW ME!

§§§

Spirit Writings: September 11, 2003; Start Time 5:15 p.m. End Time 6:10 p.m.

Me: Mum, I'm writing to you, as I feel an immense joy today. Our local priest encouraged me to continue our contact and to talk to you each time I feel the need and the desire. Right now, I feel the need to thank you. Thank you, Mum, for all your messages of love coming from the spirit world. Thank you for staying alive within us through this contact. Our faith is renewed continuously with all you are transmitting us, Mum.

I understand why it had to be this way; you had to bring us all onto the right path of light and truth. Today I accept you leaving us and passing on to the other side with much more serenity, as I know now that you brought us what was missing in our life: belief, faith, and love for others, hope for a new path, and a complete change to our current life. Mum, I am so happy that God let us have this contact; by this means, he reaches deep inside our soul. Moreover, our love for him and his son grows stronger each day that goes by, and he continuously renews our inner joy.

Through you, Mum, now a servant of God and a being of light amongst so many others, we will be able to transform ourselves and work on our belief. We respect each other's faith as long as love is the main foundation of that belief. Thank you, Mum for being near us; we are grateful to God, through Jesus, for letting you guide us.

We all love you, Mum, and because of this tremendous love, you bring us directly to God and his son. I kiss you and send you the love of each of your children, your grandchildren, and your great-grandchildren. Mum, stay near me always, and live your new life with lots of happiness and rewards. God is love, and with love, anything can exist. This contact exists because of love.

Please send God and his son eternal love for making this possible.

—Noëlette

Mum: Thank you for the beautiful words, so well written. Put them into practice each day. The Holy

Spirit, who is in you, is transforming you. Therefore, all my children, let yourselves be transformed, as I am interceding for God to send you his light and his wisdom.

Always live in the love of the Trinity, my children, who are so dear to my humble heart.

Live in peace and harmony with each other.

Where there is peace, there is love.

Where there is love, God is there.

All the energies of light will also be there.

—Mum, who will guide you always

Chapter 9

FACTS AND EVIDENCE

Spirit Writings: September 15, 2003; Start Time 12:17 p.m. End Time 12:55 p.m.

Me: Mum, can you please give me a message for Océane and George,[30] who are far from their parents and very scared about their future? Can you please advise them in their decision? I am waiting for you, Mum. Guide my hand with what you have to say to them. I send you a big kiss.

—Noël

Mum: My dear Noël, thank you for calling on me persistently in your heart. Let the holy light of Jesus Christ be the source of infinite joy within you.

To my lovely Océane and my dear George, I say this. Let your heart talk to you, as the spirit of truth resides there. Listen to it calling continuously. I have said it, and I will say it again: Do not be attached to materials, but seek spirituality instead. Hold on

---

[30]   Océane and George are a couple (family related)

divine love, earthly love, and family love. Live from the gift of the Holy Spirit in you, and remember always that it is a beautiful gift from God. Listen to the voice of the Holy Spirit, who talks to you always, and do not miss your essence as a couple. Think of making a family, as the rewards are big for those who, in love, give life to God's children, as he is inside of each of us. Always listen to his wishes in your heart.

§§§

The two I asked about in this communication had both immigrated to another country. They had a difficult time when they arrived in their new country of residence. They missed their homeland, their parents, and their siblings. Today, the two are living happily with their two children, still in their new country of residence. Their parents brought them together with their other siblings and relatives all around them. Everything turned around for them beautifully.

§§§

Spirit Writings: September 16, 2003; Start Time 11:15 a.m. End Time 11:40 a.m.

Daniel's Fortieth Birthday[31]

Mum: Noël, my child, you are inside me. My loved one, I send you my mother's blessing on this special day.

---

[31] Sibling (Fictitious name)

I know that you are still sad and in a depressive state of mind. Each time that you think of me, dry your tears and stop being so sad. Instead, think of me with a smile; peace will be in your heart, I will be present there and faithful to meet the love we bear for each other.

The new path you chose in your life, the church path, makes me happy, and your faith renews itself day by day. I am happy to see the fantastic efforts that you and the others are making. Continue in your new path; God is aware of your efforts. Pursue what you want to achieve, and it will be fruitful.

The wheel will definitely turn, my child. Be patient, and keep your faith alive, still, and patient.

§§§

Now that years have passed, I understand what she meant when she said, "The wheel will definitely turn". This particular member of the family was overseas at the time, and he was still struggling with a very difficult life with his little family. He since immigrated to another big country, and he is doing much better. The whole family is settled. They bought a brand new house, and their life has completely changed for the better compared to what they were living years before they moved. The wheel has indeed completely turned for him. Glory to God and his angels for this! What Mum said really happened without fail so far. He also has been blessed.

§§§

Spirit Writings: September 16, 2003; Start Time 5:00 p.m. End Time 5:40 p.m.

Me: Mum, sorry to call on you again. Could you send me a little message for Pascaline[32]? Monique[33] and Stephanie[34] send you all their love.

Mum: Noël, you can call me anytime. It is always great to come to you. Embrace all my children for me tightly. You are in me, and I am in you all when you follow what I convey to you to the letter.

Tell Mon[35] and Phan[36] that I love them very strongly, and tell them to continue their efforts in praying. I also pray for them and hold them in my heart.

My dearly loved Pascaline, I never cease to pray for you, because you are so fragile. Do not be sad. You seem lost. Where has your Christian faith gone, my dear? Open your heart to me, and let the spirit of love guide you. I am bound to God and to his son more than ever. You can also create that special bond between you and him (God), my child. Pray to the Holy Trinity to bring flavour back into your life.

You must no longer be desperate as you currently are, my child. God intends you to open your heart and experience a renewal. Joy, happiness, and peace will then grab your soul. It is so sweet. Let the joys of life rock you and drive you.

---

[32] Sibling (Fictitious name)

[33] My sister in France

[34] My niece in San Francisco

[35] Nickname for Monique (my sister)

[36] Nickname for Stephanie (my niece)

Ask God continually to be near you, to guide you and help you, especially when you feel exhausted. Otherwise, Satan will drag you into deeper doubt and depression. Return to God, my child. Do it for your mother, who loves you. Let only joy and serenity live in your heart now. When you are sad, I am sad also. Smile for me more, I beg of you.

§§§

Pascaline was suffering from severe depression, and her thoughts became more negative and self-harming. We were all concerned about her health and her mental state. Thank God, as Mum predicted, her life soon changed completely. She left the place where she was staying, moved to a new country, remarried, and lived a stress-free and happy life with her little family. She never went back to the state she was in before. Her life became wonderful. I give glory to God for this transformation.

§§§

Spirit Writings: September 21, 2013; Start Time 8:00 a.m. End Time 8:05 a.m.

Me: My sweet mum, how could I not engage you this day for a few small words? I would like you to remember my huge love for you. Thank you for what you do in me. I have a heavy heart from thinking that last year, you were physically present with me for my special day, but I respect God's wish to have you with him. Be always happy where you are, Mum. We are happy for you, and you soothe our grief. The days pass, but you are present in our hearts. I love you, Mum. Have I said this enough? I embrace you strongly and send you thousands of kisses on behalf of all your children and grandchildren.

—Noëlette

Mum: Noël, my child –

This took place on my birthday. I had to interrupt the communication, as someone who was not aware of my contact with Mum came into the room.

§§§

Spirit Writings: September 22, 2013; Start Time 9:55 a.m. End Time 10:40 a.m.

Me: Mum, if all is well today, can you send me a little message? My apologies for yesterday. I could not let you convey me the message you wanted to give me. However, you have been in my heart throughout the day, as you know. I send you rose petals on an ocean of love, Mum.

—Your girl who loves you beyond the oceans, Noëlette

Mum: Noël, my child, receive my blessing and the blessing of our merciful Father, from his son, our saviour and lord, Jesus Christ, and the blessing of our holy Mother Mary, a wonderful beauty.

I was happy to feel the immense love that we share in perfect harmony with each other. Always keep this spirit of love for your brothers and sisters, Noël, and be happy for all that God has sent you. There have been moments of great joy and moments of great sadness. He sent you these projects continuously to

test your faith. He tests you in your moments of happiness to see if you forget him while intoxicated with good feelings. He also tests you in hard times to see if you distance yourself from him. Stay attentive during each event, and remember that if he wants it this way, you must surrender yourself completely to him and his will. His love is vast and endless. Always be present when he calls. Your efforts are great in the eyes of God and his beloved son. Continue living this way, and I know you can do much more.

May peace always live in you, Noël. Live at peace with the certainty that I exist in a wonderful world where there is only love. Our God of supreme love enables us to live around him and in his love; therefore, everything is accomplished with amazement, happiness, and deep joy. Have a happy heart, and may the light of the Holy Spirit live there. May the miraculous presence of the spirit of wisdom, love, vision, charity, and peace constantly renew this feeling.

§§§

Spirit Writings: September 27, 2003; Start Time 4:00 p.m. End Time 4:35 p.m.

Me: Mum, your picture is right before my eyes. It's the one we took of you lying in your coffin. Even though it was a sad time, I'm happy, because I know you're still alive—simultaneously far away but close to us because God gave us this way to contact each other. Can you tell me why this magic is possible with me and not with others? Do you and the others in heaven want to drive me towards certain goals through these messages? I know that they have greatly helped us change our lives, but I have asked myself all week, "Do we have to keep these messages just for ourselves?" If you do not mind, Mum, with the agreement of the Being of Light, please advise me.

Mum: Noël, I am very pleased with this resumed contact. Be at peace always. My beloved good girl, it is possible for you to communicate with me because you received a gift while you were still in the womb. This gift slept in you throughout your life until the day I caused you to put it into practice. Throughout your life, you will now see and feel things that others may not. However, you need use this gift to do good always. Do not ever consider using it for an advantage or for material ends; especially do not plan to enrich yourself with it. Rather, use it to enrich yourself and others at the time God chooses. For now, continue our communication with love humility, and simplicity. The messages are for a specific purpose: letting believers and non-believers know the truth about what resurrection is. In fact, we never really die; we leave our physical body and return home in our spiritual state of being. We only passed to the other side. Tell the people around you about this, and read my messages to all, particularly for those who still do not believe in them. Do not give up. I am with you in all your endeavours. Mum is proud to see you overcoming your doubts. Continue likewise, my children. I am always with

you. Let the Spirit of God always have a prominent place in your heart.

Me: Thank you, Mum, for your good advice. I will catch up soon. Kisses.

—Noël

§§§

Spirit Writings: September 29, 2003; Start Time 11:00 a.m. End Time 11:30 a.m.

Me: Mum, how could I not think about you on this day that reminds us of our physical separation exactly four months ago? Yesterday, Paula[37] and I reminded each other of those hard times. We miss you so much, as the house is empty without you, Mum. I want to apologize, Mum, and say sorry for all the times I have been heartless with you. We do not realise what harm we can do to someone in his or her lifetime on earth. Remorse plagues our souls by telling us repeatedly, "If only you knew …" If I knew, Mum, that you would not have spent this year with me, I would have avoided doing things that caused you pain. Forgive me, Mum, and pray for me and all your children."

Mum: Noële Aux Quatre Vents[38] do not be sad today. Mum is always present near you. You do not have to ask me for forgiveness. I give you love today. My love helps God forgive you for your sins on earth. My children, have no fear; we are all sinners before God, but try to redeem yourself throughout your life. The

---

[37] Sister (Fictitious name)

[38] Nickname of mine meaning "Noële of Four Winds".

problem is that you do not know your life's duration. Each passing day, think only of doing good deeds. I love you with my entire soul. Remember, tomorrow is never guaranteed. Always look for the face of Christ to be reflected in your brothers and sisters in Christ. See you soon, my daughter.

§§§

Spirit Writings: October 1, 2003; Start Time 1:05 p.m. End Time 2:00 p.m.

Me: Dear Mum, as I asked you this morning at Mass, I will ask you again if you want to send me a little message for Lydia.[39] Today is her birthday, moreover, let me know if it is possible for Dominic[40] (who passed over at two weeks old), Arlette (our sister who passed over at the age of two), Sylvain (our brother who passed over at four months old) to send us messages. If so, can you ask Dominic if he would pass a message through you or directly to me? I will also take this opportunity to ask you to embrace all three of them for all of us, because they are in our hearts more than ever. Be happy, Mum, and comfort us by letting us know. I am at your service and the services of the highest power.

Ten minutes passed without any response, and I almost lost hope.

♥ ♥ ♥

---

[39]   Sister (Fictitious name)
[40]   Nephew (Fictitious name)

Dominic[41]: Mum, it's I— Dominic. I am a messenger from God, an angel who watches and protects you constantly. Be happy for me, Mum. I know you and Dad are in deep pain. You cannot imagine the immensity of my love for you. I am with you forever, Mum. More angels surround me, and we rescue many souls in distress. My life here is so full. God is good, and he constantly gives us love. Always pray to him, my sweet mother. I will be closer to you from now on. I am in you mum, dad, brother, and sister; you are under my protective wings of light.

♥ ♥ ♥

Me: Dominic, my celestial angel. Your mum sends her infinite love. Be happy always. Protect us always with your power. You will remain in our hearts, Dominic. Thank you, Mum for calling Dominic to send a message for his mum. She receives a great gift from heaven. Thank you, Mum. I embrace you tightly. You made us experience many emotions today, as tears of joy followed this amazing connection.

♥ ♥ ♥

You can imagine the questions my relatives asked after this message. They called me crazy, and some said that I was playing with their feelings. Others pointed their fingers at me and told me to stop this blasphemy. One family member asked how a baby who died so young could write or speak. I told this relative that Dominic has grown up since then, as in heaven, you don't remain a baby; you proceed through

---

[41]   My nephew (Fictitious name)

spiritual life, and he would grow into a teenager and then a grown male angel. The relative laughed at me. Some members of my family told me to stop all this nonsense because I kept making a fool of myself. It was so hard to share the messages with them. I was ridiculed.

§§§

Spirit Writings: October 2, 2003; Start Time 11:05 a.m. End Time 12:25 p.m.

Me: "Dear Mum, I call again from the bottom of my heart to let you in, and wish to clear up the misunderstanding others experienced from yesterday's message. Was it Dominic who wrote me the message or did the magic happen through you? Dominic's dad does not believe that his son was able to send him a message. He wondered how Dominic could learn to write to him, as he was a baby when he passed on to the other side. My heart was deeply hurt by so many misunderstandings, but my faith remains intact. I am not like St Thomas. My heart revealed many deep and strong things, and I feel the spirit of light without the slightest doubt. The light dwells in me and gives me strength to continue approaching you, despite the issues and words that hurt me. However, I accept the belief or disbelief of each family member because I know that there will be tests on my path. I am ready for anything with the love of Christ. I kiss you, Mum, and please embrace Dominic, Arlette, and Sylvain and all other members of the family for me.

—*Your daughter, Noëlette*

Mum: Noël, my daughter, I'm sad to see the disagreement with the love that binds two beings, one on earth and

one in heaven. You have not found the true value of this wonderful gift from God yet. You still do not know how to appreciate the incredible opportunity you have with all these heavenly messages. Where is your faith in the invisible—in the power of love?

For the message from Dominic, I only have to create a channel to him with love so that he can send you what he feels. It was possible for me to relay to you the message because of the immensity of the love he feels for his mother. There are no barriers or obstacles when love exists.

Do you think you would see me the way I looked when I left you? Well, you are wrong. Everything is possible because of God's love; therefore, stop thinking of Dominic as a child. Imagine him as a handsome man with curly hair, as children grow and become adult angels. However, some things are not permissible for me to say. This sounds illogical and incredible, but the sky is magical. Everything is possible through the immense love with which God leads us. If it helps you to understand what happens when we communicate, know that we can travel many distances in the mind. We can feel and hear everything, and we are magical as we serve our one and only God, our creator. May peace be within you, Noël, and in all.

§§§

Spirit Writings: October 8, 2003; Start Time 6:05 p.m. End Time 7:00 p.m.

Me: Mum, I address these words to you with great tenderness and love. I entrust you with my visit to a priest, who has encouraged me once again to keep our communication, as they are messages of love. However, I think you already know this. I wanted to say thank you, Mum, for remaining with us through these initial moments of contact. I thank God and his son, Jesus Christ, with all my heart and soul for giving us this wonderful gift, priceless gift of love.

Your children always think of you, Mum, and you are always in our hearts. We still feel your absence, as we never expected such a misfortune would happen. However, luckily we have this wonderful chance to know you are happy and the chance to receive messages from you. Some people think I am crazy, but I persevere in my faith in this gift. I think, Mum, as the priest said so well, that by grace and love, anything is possible. I love you, Mum, and so do all your children. This love unites us beyond physical death, and we continue talking as before, without any barriers, Mum.

Thank you so much for interceding for us with God, his beloved son, the Virgin Mary, St Joseph, and all the saints and angels and archangels. If you can, intercede with Archangel Michaël for us so that the devil cannot approach anyone of us. Finally, thank you, Mum, for praying unceasingly for us. We are reaping the fruits. Always protect each of your children, grandchildren, and great-grandchildren. We will all carry you in our hearts and tell you we love you forever. One day, we will all find ourselves in the house of our Holy Father with his beloved son. Offer him our eternal love, Mum, and ask them to enlighten us continually by sending us the Holy Spirit.

Convey our love to all those we know who are with you, including Dominic, Arlette, and Sylvain, who are in our hearts now and always.

Mum: Noël, thank you for meeting with me. I am happy to see you so calm. Continue to follow the path on which God leads you. You will reap fruit in abundance. You are under my protection, and my love for you will never end. By living out the gift God gave you, you will tell him you love him back. Do not shrink from even the worst trials, as they are from him. Do not hesitate to act for God in all circumstances, even the most humiliating ones. His love for each of us is endless, and he is just and merciful to everyone. Do not be ashamed to speak in his name and proclaim his goodness always.

From Gerda, your mum forever.

§§§

Mum's statement that "you will reap fruit in abundance" came true, as I am now an Australian citizen, and my two children and their dad as well. My hard work paid off, and I finally bought a beautiful house in Australia. I raised my two children on my own, struggling as a single mum after my divorce and today my daughter is about to turn twenty-one. She is doing well in her career as a dental assistant and would love to succeed locally and internationally in her modelling career as well. My son is nearly fifteen. His career objective is to become a lawyer. He is still in high school and is a nice handsome and so respectful teenager. I am proud of my achievements and my children's achievements. The fact that I have published this book and you are reading it is also a great accomplishment. Lord, bless me, my generation, all who are reading these pages, and our descendants. I am so blessed. Amen.

Thanks, Mum, as without your guidance, I would not be where I am today. I would never have accomplished what I have so far. I am grateful to the universe for all these blessings on my family and myself.

Chapter 10

WE CREATE OUR OWN HEAVEN OR HELL

Spirit Writings: October 12, 2003; Start Time 7:10 p.m. End Time 7:45 p.m.

Me: Mum, love of our life, I wish you much happiness and a fruitful life where you are. I send you all my love, not to mention the love of your other children. I have not forgotten you, and you remain in our hearts. Kisses from Noël. If you want to tell me something, I am here, waiting for you.

Mum: Noël, thank you for your love, and thank the others for keeping me alive in their hearts. Remember to keep the most important place for God, our Holy Father. Give him each moment you have available, for he is waiting to welcome you with tenderness and love.

May peace always live in you, my dear children. Direct your life to paradise, where I await you and those who help you. I will bring you into the love of God.

**Be happy, my children, and accumulate wealth in heaven.
Mum intercedes and prays for you constantly. Love,
my children, is the largest treasure you can possess.
May your life be a road coloured with love.
I'm sending you my love.**

§§§

One member of our family, Joseph,[42] did some bad
things in life, as many humans do. He was a gambler, a
smoker, and an alcoholic. On top of this, he had several
affairs after he married his wife, and hits his spouse nearly
every day. His wife stopped working because of the marks
all over her body. Life around this man was like hell. At the
end of most days, he fought with his wife after losing his
wages at the casino, and his wife was always struggling to
pay for the rent, utilities, food, and so forth. Moreover, his
children never really saw him, as he departed home early
in the morning and came back late at night. Therefore, the
children grew up in a very tense atmosphere. The beatings
never stopped, and the children eventually started to work
to help their mum run the house, as their dad was still
gambling at the casino and horse races. Everything went into
it: his wages, his lump sums, his superannuation, and even
the deposit money that his wife gave him for the purchase of
their first house. Therefore, they eventually lost that house.
With my own eyes, I saw the sad and difficult life his family
went through because of his behaviour. Watching their
life going downwards made me hate all types of gambling
update. Their life was full of torment, and the wife was

---

42   Relative Fictitious name

a tough woman who never gave up. She kept fighting to survive and gave the children an education, despite their dad never being there for them. Slowly but surely, this woman saved money with her children's help, and she bought a land and built a brand-new house. She knew she couldn't trust her husband, so she did everything without him this time. Each of the children helped with what they could, as life was not easy in their homeland during those days, and they were all having hard times back then. That strong woman got her house in the end where she stayed until she passed on to the other side. Thank you, Lord, for this blessing. When I asked Mum if she met Joseph where she was and if he was okay, she revealed that he wasn't in a very good place. In other words, he wasn't near her. He was likely far away from her, in a darker place—a very unpleasant one.

I once had a message from beyond through a well-known medium who said that this man came forward to say that he was sorry for all the pain he had caused his loved ones. Even though his family was not happy about the wrong things he did, they never hated him deep inside. They all loved him. In fact, when this man was sober, he was the nicest and most caring man on the planet. He adored playing with his grandkids and spending time with his loved ones on weekends. He enjoyed cooking for his family every Sunday. Everyone in the family wished that he could change and be a better person, but in the end, who were we to judge or to blame him for what he did? Were we sinless? No, we were not, then or now! Each of us has an individual path, and it is not our duty to judge anyone on earth. Moreover, we need to experience good and bad to grow on our spiritual path. The preceding story will help you understand the following conversation.

§§§

Spirit Writings: October 16, 2003; Start Time 6:45 p.m.
End Time 7: p.m.

Me: Mum, are you near me?
Mum: Yes, Noël, I am always near you and all others.
Me: We miss you so much, Mum—all of us.
Mum: I am sorry to cause so much sorrow and pain. I would like you to be happier.
Me: Mum, yesterday was Joseph's birthday, and we thought of him deeply. We wish him well.
Mum: You never lost us, Noël. We are still alive in your hearts.
Me: Can Joseph influence his family or the rest of us and act upon our thoughts?
Mum: Yes, Noël. You have to choose which path to follow, but I am here with Arlette [sister], Sylvain [brother], Dominic[43] [nephew], and the Holy Spirit to help keep you from falling into the abyss.
Me: What can we do to counteract the bad influence, Mum?
Mum: Pray, my children. God never abandons one of his sheep.
Me: Mum, I love you. We all love you dearly, and we wish for the Holy Spirit to be in us each day of our life.
Mum: Yes, Noël, give him your entire life, and he will fill it with love.
Mum loves you.
Be happy in the love of God and his son.

---

[43] Fictitious name

§§§

I think that when Joseph passed over, he went to a very difficult place wherein he had to face his conscience, and he had the chance to face the wrongs of his life and repent. I pray for him every day, to ask for help and forgiveness so that he will turn himself towards the light. I hope that after all these years, Joseph is in a much better place. I rarely see him in my dreams, but recently I dreamed of him embracing me, and I felt love between us. He presented himself through a medium once and gave me a message for his family, asking for their forgiveness. However, I have not heard of him since. I always wish him well and send him my love, light, blessings, and prayers. I guess Joseph was just a lost soul. Despite what Mum said, I hope he has found his way to the light by now. I deeply loved him, no matter what he did.

§§§

I love you, Joseph, now and always. The members of our family and yours also love you. When you lose those precious to your heart, you become aware of how much you valued them. We miss you in the family for sure. Moreover, we love you now and forever. You too, Mum: I love you forever.

§§§

Spirit Writings: October 21, 2003; Start Time 6:10 p.m. End Time 6:35 p.m.

Mum: My child, continue to follow the path wherein God leads you. Follow him without any hesitation,

Noël; he is the light of the world. He loves us with pure and deep love. Every day spent with him fills us with wonderful feelings of love. Our brother, Jesus Christ, is so good; gentleness emanates from him, the light of the world, equal to his Father. Noël, give yourself totally to him; his love for each of us is infinite.

Continue your journey to Jesus Christ and his wife.[44] Listen to the holy words in the house of the Lord, and always be blessed, my children.

Let the Holy Spirit comfort you, my children, and may your heart welcome and share Christ's love.

§§§

Spirit Writings: October 25, 2003; Start Time 3:00 p.m. End Time 3:30 p.m.

Me: Dear Mum, I just read a great book called "La Troisième Oreille: À l'écoute de l'au-delà" *from author Marcel Belline. It explained another type of communication known as clairaudience between a son in the spirit world with his father who was still alive; he could hear his son talking to him. It is magical, and I remembered that you told me everything was magic in paradise. Could you enlighten me on this?"*

Mum: Noël I am in you as this son is in his father. Don't you feel my continuous presence in you? When we love, nothing dies. Everything is still the same, as love is light. Light attracts light and unites people.

---

[44] The church

Me: Can we meet in dreams, Mum? I have dreamed of you
often lately, beautiful and smiling. Could you visit me in
dreams more often?

Mum: I'll see you soon and talk to you one night. Go to
sleep in peace, and I will visit you.

§§§

Spirit Writings: October 27, 2003; Start Time 7:40 p.m.
End Time 8:20 p.m.

When I asked Mum tonight about how she felt the
moment she left her physical body, she said the following:

"I knew when I was approaching the end of earthly
life, because it is a strange feeling when the time comes.
I suffered a lot but for a good cause. All suffering is
recognized, and accepting it makes us humble before
God. I heard you. All your comforting and encouraging
words and your prayers helped me greatly. I felt your
caresses, your kisses, and your hands in mine; I noticed
every step, tear, and laugh. I was in perfect communion
with you, but you could not doubt it. As a relief, I left
my body. It was deliverance—a gift and a blessing—
because it was so peaceful and beautiful. However, there
are things that I cannot tell you, as none of you would
understand. Soak up all of my light."

§§§

Spirit Writings: October 29, 2003; Start Time 5:55 a.m.
End Time 6:25 a.m.

I received the following message from a friend, Clyde,[45] who is in the spirit world. It was for his son.

"My son,
I am present with you.
Every day that passes,
I am happy.
Do not be sad for me.
Just live your life.
I love you very strongly.
I am in you and you in me.
Above all, we are one.
I love you.
Your dad loves you and cares about you.
—C

§§§

After my family members heard this message, they were greatly agitated. They thought I was going more crazy, as most would not accept this message from our friend. People think that when we cross over, we are the same. They think that we remain a certain way, as we bring with us all we liked to do here, all we used to be, but we are different in our feelings. We are more aware of love around us and love for the people we left. Those who cross over would certainly change their perception on life itself, as what they used to believe does not exist in the way they thought it would; what they learned is nothing in comparison to what they experience in heaven or the other dimensions. Over there,

---

[45] Fictitious name (died tragically in a road accident).

there is no limit, no end, and no time. In addition, people are no longer in the same physical body, as they are in a spiritual body. We will see things differently, act differently, and talk differently, as we will have reached a higher level of awareness. That is why it is difficult for most of us on earth to recognize a particular person when he or she comes back to us. The loved one may talk differently and act differently, as he or she is completely spiritual and in a new body that shines, as it's made of pure light.

§§§

Spirit Writings: November 4, 2003; Start Time 00:58 a.m. End Time 2:02 a.m.

Me: Mum, are you in my thoughts? I need your help and your wisdom.

Mum: Noël, I am happy to meet with you. May the joy of the Holy Spirit live within you forever. Mum is always present among you. May the peace of Jesus be with you all.

Me: Mum, excuse me, as I have not left a note recently. That is what I was wondering about the responsibility that falls to me in the family about the messages. Sometimes, I wonder if the messages torment them instead of bringing them peace of mind.

Mum: Noël, I know it is not an easy responsibility for you to carry, and each message has its interpretation. The messages enlighten you, and your faith has increased; the changes occurring in you are the fruits of the Holy Spirit. Your brothers and sisters

do not experience the life you do, Noël; share the light with them.

Noël, tell everyone not to be sad anymore. You should think about yourselves more; think about living on earth and what you can accomplish for God in his son, Jesus Christ.

Your love for God must exceed the love you have for me, my children. Live in the present and the future, holy and humbly.

§§§

Mum explained the following after I asked whether people could repent and get out of hell:

No, nobody comes back from hell. They should have repented at the time the Being of Light gave them the opportunity to do so. Imagine that there are souls in purgatory, who aim to free themselves and evolve into higher realms; they feel remorseful, so they learn again how to forgive, care for others, and love each other. However, hell is total darkness with self-harm, distress, torment, pain, and suffering, as people there refuse repentance, light, love, and everything good. Heaven is total bliss, with infinite love and light. Be aware that light and darkness flows both ways. Cease to torture yourselves, my children, with those things; think of the present or of where you would like to be, and I hope you will choose this light. Act accordingly, therefore, to come to heaven, where God has already reserved your place. If you think your loved ones might be in hell, pray that the angels around the edge of hell mitigate the suffering, because hell is eternal death. Think of your

children, your brothers and sisters, and yourself, and decide to live an eternal life in heaven because of these beautiful messages.

I think that mum was saying we create our own hell and heaven. In other words, how we live our life right now determines our life in the hereafter. Therefore, if you want to live a wonderful life in heaven, you had better make your own heaven on earth.

Chapter 11

CHALLENGING TIMES

One of my close relative, Paul,[46] was suddenly nearly 75 per cent paralysed. I was very close to him. I had a lot of respect for him and did not know how to help him in these difficult times. He saw several specialists; they all said the problem he had was inoperable in our homeland, Mauritius Island. They said he would become totally paralysed, and there was nothing they could do to prevent it. I followed my intuition and asked Mum to guide me on the right path to help him. I received the guidance to advise him to visit our family doctor, who gave Paul the information of an excellent neurosurgeon overseas. Paul had to have an operation immediately, as he was unable to walk properly. It was a difficult time indeed for Paul's wife, Rose,[47] who had to organize her husband's surgery overseas. They both had to face the unexpected trauma and their two children's confusion. I was not over the physical death of mum yet when this big stress came up: trying to help Paul find

[46] A very close relative (Fictitious name)

[47] Fictitious name

healing and get better to support his family again. This new trauma affected me a lot, as Paul was a family member dear to my heart. I was depressed and stressed, so I asked Mum for guidance regarding their life.

§§§

Spirit Writings: November 23, 2003; Start Time 11:15 a.m. End Time 11:25 a.m.

Me: Mum, it's been a while since I have written to you. You should certainly know this family's torment. Mum, help them endure this ordeal.

Mum: Noël, my child, don't give up hope. I am here.

Me: Mum, I love you very dearly. Do not ever forget it.

Mum: Noël, I will never forget. I know the immensity of your love.

Me: Mum, protect Paul.

Mum: Noël, he is already under my protection.

Me: Mum, give them hope that it's not as bad as we think.

Mum: Think about the children, Noël. Have faith, and pray.

Me: Thank you, Mum.

Mum: Courage to you, Noël, and to this family as well.

§§§

Spirit Writings: December 2, 2003; Start Time 6:40 p.m. End Time 7:15 p.m.

Me: Mum, it's been such a long time since I have written you. I feel guilty. I wanted to take a step back in light of what all the others have felt against our messages. Then, as you know, a whirlpool of events upset my life. Mum, I write you tonight because I feel the very strong need not to find comfort but to remind you that you are still present in my thoughts now, more than ever. You are in peace, Mum, away from all of these concerns of the earth. I love you, Mum.

—Your daughter, Noëlette

Noël, my child, have courage and be strong. Regarding Paul[48] and his wife, I will remove from their path all peril. I will lead them to the right destination. Help Paul and wife in this test. Remind them to have faith that the impossible is possible for God. I pray for you, Noël, and this family. I know the size of your faith. God will fervently give you anything for which you ask. He hears your prayers, and your requests make miracles.

Noël, your faith protects everyone in the family and everyone surrounding you. Never neglect the one and only God. Remain in communion with me. Take good care of yourself, Noël. I love you very deeply.

§§§

The day was approaching for Paul and wife, Rose, to fly overseas to have his complex operation. The neurosurgeon warned them that there was 50 per cent chance that he might come back home in a wheel chair totally paralysed, so he should have everything organized for this eventuality ahead of time. They prepared for that situation, but deep

---

[48]   Family member (Fictitious name)

inside, we prayed to all the angels, archangels, God, Mother Mary, and Jesus Christ to help him and his family in this tribulation. I was sad for the two children, as they did not understand what was really happening being still young. The parents did not want to alarm them, and Rose stood tall with courage for herself and her family. What a very courageous woman she was in that very difficult time!

Husband and wife were finally preparing to leave for a first consultation with the neurosurgeon overseas. I asked Mum for her complete protection, and I was not scared, as I had the feeling that everything would be fine for them and that Paul would walk back home like a newborn man after the surgery. I had strong faith in that. I believed in his total recovery.

Before this couple left for the appointment, I asked Mum for a message as follows:

Spirit Writings: December 8, 2003; Start Time 5:15 a.m. End Time 5:50 a.m.

Me: Mum, our protector from heaven, may heaven itself be on this couple's side –as you know—as they head towards the meeting for the first steps to success on Paul's surgery. Mum, are they on the right path? Is this the way you wanted them to go, Mum? If you cannot tell me much, at least give me a sign that I guided them on the right path—the path wherein God and his son lead us. Thank you, Mum. I love you very dearly, and you are in the deepest part of my heart.
—Noëlette.

Mum: Tell them to go with confidence from now on, my child. We heard your prayers, and we are ready to

help Paul. Our Holy Father and his son, Jesus, heard your prayers join with the prayers of everyone who prayed for him. Without ever witnessing a miracle, Noël, you believe, and your faith will do many things.

Continue your journey, Noël. If you had not already been on this journey for some time, you would not have had so much courage, and you would not have been enlightened to this point.

The Holy Spirit is in you, Noël, as you ask him into your life without end. Accomplish the missions he gives you: the missions of unity, charity, suffering, reconciliation, love, and hope in Christ's love.

Do not be scared, Noël, and follow the doors that open without knocking. God loves you and all my children. Accept suffering and tests as an offering, and praise God always. I love you all. Pray always.

§§§

Spirit Writings: December 18, 2003; Start Time 6:15 p.m. End Time 7:00 p.m.

Me: My dearest mother, whom I love so much, I wish you happiness and peace. You know my state of mind and my fears. You also know the distress Paul has recently experienced. Mum, thank you for all that you do for all of us. I thank God through Jesus, his son, for showing us his great love through this ordeal. You certainly know our future, Mum, and I know that whatever happens, you will be here to help us. If our pain is useful, then I accept this pain, and I never will turn away from God and his son because of it. I love you very much, Mum. Your children are wonderful and caring, and they share in this suffering with me. They help me hold this cross to bear. I know you are present among us and that you attend to these gestures of love between us. Mum, we love you deeply, and you will stay forever in our hearts.

—*Noël Aux Quatre Vents, as you called me so well*

Mum: Noël, your message moved me. You are in me, and I am in you, through this union of love. You have made the right decisions for Paul and his family. Just have faith in God's goodness, Noël. Continue your efforts on the path. You will need much courage on arrival at the destination. Noël, do not forget, my child, that God recognizes all suffering. He allows us to experience suffering because he loves us. Moreover, his love is immeasurable. Know that it is a great love, and you will know that he holds you in these distressing times. You will understand one day why this suffering is in your life; more importantly, you will understand how it affects and unites the entire family. Have faith in God, my children; he is the Eternal Father who gave us love through his son, Jesus Christ. Pray, my children. Mum loves you all eternally. I am in your heart more than ever. Always be ready for each call from God, and answer it without trying to understand. Noël, say yes to the call with your eyes closed. Follow our saviour, the Lord Jesus Christ, blindly. Offer Paul consolation in these painful but essential moments. You are contributing to a new land without even realizing it.

Me: Thank you, Mum, for this wonderful message. We love you so dearly. All of your children and grandchildren send you their deep love and thank you for all the guidance you bring us from heaven.

—Noël

§§§

Spirit Writings: January 7, 2004; Start Time 3:40 p.m. End Time 4:07 p.m.

Me: Mum, it is with emotion that I resume writing and send you these few words of love from us all. We wish you a good and holy year, Mum, wherever you are. We send you all our love; you will always remain in our hearts. We love you very deeply, Mum. Are you with us? Are you happy to see us all gathered in your memory?

Mum: Mum loves you always, my children. To see you reunited fills me with joy. Always live like this, my children and grandchildren. You are beautiful to watch from above. I wish you all peace. Do not be sad for me. I am satisfied. Mum sees you all and loves you all, and love is eternal. Have a holy new year. Watching you so united fills me with joy. I hold all of you tenderly. As Christ dwells in you, I remain in you all, and all of you remain in me.

—Gerda, your mum forever

§§§

Spirit Writings: January 10, 2004; Start Time 8:50 a.m. End Time 9:37 a.m.

This was the day scheduled for Paul to have his surgery.

Me: Mum, as you already know, Paul and his wife followed the path outlined for the perfect success of his operation today. I trust in God's goodness and mercy. Thank you for helping all of us from above, Mum. We have all been happy to reunite as one in your home, and we are happy to know that we gave you great pleasure. Even if you were not with us physically, Mum, you were among us. We felt your presence stronger than ever. To you, our protective spirit in heaven, we renew our eternal love. If you want to send us a note, I am at your disposal.

—*Noël*

All Mum's children, even the overseas ones, decided to reunite in Mum's house for Christmas 2003 and New Year's 2004 celebrations and to be together for the first time without Mum, celebrating in her house.

Mum: My children, Mum was happy to see you reunited. I am with you every passing moment. Have no fear; I will always protect you. May there always be love and peace between you. Mum loves you all. Never doubt that. Take the path of holiness, my children and grandchildren. I am with you every day of your lives. Noël, my Noële Aux Quatre Vents have courage; we are all with you. Guard your faith and believe in what you feel. We are protecting you from above. Thanks to the strength of your prayers, a higher power will come on Paul and his wife and children. We are in communion with you in prayer. My children and grandchildren, receive the blessing of the Father,

Son, and Holy Spirit. I bless you all too. The grace of heaven blessed your mum to be near you all. I love you. I will always love you. I have never left you and will never forsake you. Always listen to your heart; I speak to you there without fail.

—Gerda, your mother eternally

§§§

Moreover, as Mum predicted, everything went well for Paul. There were no complications, even though the surgery went for several hours. Paul came out a new man. His fear that he could not walk was of no more concern. In addition, his fear of not being a man anymore disappeared. Thank you, Lord. That was a real miracle, as this risky operation was so dangerous and delicate. However, thanks to the Lord, everything went smoothly. Paul's re-education in how to walk as he regained feeling also went well. Jesus Christ, thank you. That was a miracle. He went back home happy. To this day, Paul is walking fine and has not suffered any more paralysis. Glory to God. Amen. Paul was blessed.

Mum: Our Lord Jesus never stops talking to you, my children, in the silence of your hearts. Listen to what he says and take action. Our Lord loves you, sinners that you are. He rejoices at any sheep he finds, and you could be the sheep that Jesus holds in his arms again. Paul, today, is one of these sheep.

To answer a question regarding whether anyone in the family could write to her, Mum replied:

Yes, Noël, we simply need this love connection. Be pure in your soul. With our heavenly Father, everything is possible, my children.

§§§

Spirit Writings: January 30, 2004; Start Time 9:15 p.m. End Time 10:15 p.m.

I expressed thanks for Paul's surgical success.

Me: Mum, it is with great emotion that I take up my pen tonight to send you these words. I feel so much need and desire that nothing can stop me from sending you this message of love from the depths of my heart. Thank you, Mum, for your prayers of intercession for Paul, his family, and all of us. As you predicted, everything went miraculously well. By the grace of God, the Father of Mercy; the ardent love that Jesus, his son, leads us towards; and the strength of his spirit of love, everything developed smoothly, Mum.
The doors opened without requiring us to knock on them. Send all our thanks to God our Father, his son of perfect love, and the Holy Mother, queen of heaven and earth as well as to all the saints and angels. Please intercede so that Paul is free from all hurt and that he has a smooth recovery from his operation. Mum, you are in communion with me and will always remain in it. You will stay warm in my heart. You have a special place there, and so do God, Jesus, Mary, and Joseph as well as all the saints, angels, and those who are dear to us. I am with Miguel.[49] As you

---

[49]   Fictitious name for sibling

know, Mum, he always sends you his eternal love. If you want to send me a message, I remain at your disposal, my darling mum.

—*Noële Aux Quatre Vents*

Mum: Noël, my child, I am pleased by this resumed contact. I am proud of you, my daughter. You demonstrated to everyone how courageous you were. Paul and his family were courageous as well. God did not abandon you, my children, and he never will. Keep your whole faith in him; he loves you infinitely. Listen to his appeal inside your heart always, Noël, to you and the whole family. Praise the Lord for this wonderful grace, my dear children.

I am proud of you all. I love you all. The force between you is an example of sharing, of unity, and of love. Your sincere prayers have all been heard. Never break this chain of prayers for your brothers and sisters of the earth and beyond. Be happy to have this time together, my children. Miguel, my child, I love you too.

Me: Thanks, Mum, for your message. You remain in the hearts of all your children, sons-in-law, daughters-in-law, and grandchildren. We embrace you all in love, Mum.

—*Noël*

Chapter 12

MESSAGES AT HIGHER LEVELS

Spirit Writings: February 8, 2004; Start Time 3:25 p.m.
End Time 4:25 p.m.

*Me: Mum, you are in our hearts today more than ever. How
could we forget that it is your birthday, Mum? You are
and will always remain in all of our hearts. I am the
spokesperson for all your children to wish you a happy
birthday where you are, Mum. I wish for peace, joy, and
love to exist always in your new home. We hold you close to
our heart and remind you of our eternal love, our motherly
courage, and our heavenly protector. Mum, I am going to
hand my pen to Pascal.*[50] *If you have a message for all of
us, guide his hand to convey your wise words. We embrace
you very tight, Mum. I passed my pen to Pascal, who is
expecting a word from you, if you do not mind. We love
you, Mum. We all love you very much.*

---

[50] Fictitious name for sibling

There was no response.

Me: Mum, is there a problem? Can you be in contact with Pascal?

Mum: Yes, Noël, I can communicate without fail, but you have to be receptive to the line of love that binds me to you all. Tell all the children that I am always with all of you. I love you. I have not forgotten you. While I am in your heart, I will always be near you. I never stop speaking to your heart, and I send you signs of my presence among you. Be attentive to every call that I make.

Noël, thank you for sending me your love. I am still as close to you as you wish, my dear children. Stop crying for me. I have a life full of love. Be holy and pure, my children. Think of yourself and purify your soul, for you have already acquired your place here, my children. Mum loves you infinitely. Pascal, may this sadness disappear from your heart. Only allow joy to live there.

I will find you one evening.

—Mum

§§§

Pascal was very depressed and still felt so much pain about Mum's departure. So much sorrow inhabited him. He was unable to find his way or to let Mum go. Now he understands that Mum never left and still surrounds him in all his decisions. In addition, now I understand what Mum said about being on the same receptive line of love; we need both to be at the same level of frequency to be able to communicate. We on earth tune in to a higher frequency while those in the spirit world lower theirs and both meet in between their two worlds. It takes efforts from both to be at such level to communicate. The magic happens there, as we can communicate and interact. Only at this compatible level are we able to tune in and receive to their messages. Moreover, we need to have complete trust in what we are receiving.

I received the following message while asking Mum if some of the people we knew were in heaven. (For privacy reasons, I will not mention the specific names here).

Noël, all the names you mentioned are happy where they are. They have their place in the house of our Heavenly Father and the universe. They protect the ones they love and never forsake them. They are still in their hearts. They will remain present among their loved ones. Pray to your protectors, my children. They intercede with our heavenly mother without ceasing. Your dear friends and family whom you buried in a grave are not there; they are always by your side. As long as there is a thread of love between two beings, their connection remains.

Isn't it beautiful to know that our loved ones are still around us and that as long as love exists between us, nothing can separate us? It is such an amazing gift to be aware of this. I thank my mum for sharing this.

§§§

Spirit Writings: February 29, 2004; Start Time 8:40 p.m. End Time 9:30 p.m.

On the day of this communication, I brought my two children, Caroline and Loïc, to the cemetery in the morning with me.

Me: My dearest Mama, it's been a while since I last wrote to you. I apologize if you were expecting a word from me; you know how eventful my life is. However, you also know that I will not forget you for even a moment; you haunt my dreams every night. It is so great to be able to dream of you. It is a grace, because it allows me to see you and talk to you. Dreaming is so beautiful, isn't it, Mum? Come visit me as much as you like. My heart overflows with joy every time I see you before me in such dreams. I love you, Mum, and I will not forget you. As I said today on your grave, "You are in me". Thank you, Mum, for protecting us. None of your children will forget you. You remain in our hearts. You have been our mother on earth, and you will remain Mum beyond this earth. We will meet one day again beyond this earth. All your children kiss you and hold you closely. You are in all of us, Mum. We all love you. Thank you, Mum, for being constantly present among us and for making this clear through signs. Thank you, Mum, for this testimony of love, and thank God through his son, Jesus Christ, for all these graces.

—Noël

Mum: I am glad to read your message, Noël. Noël, my daughter, I only want all my children to be happy. Mum prays for you without stopping. Repent, my children, and receive forgiveness. Make progress on the earth for your future life in heaven. Love your brothers and sisters of the earth, even those whom you would like to hate. Love your enemies, and come to the aid of all who need your support. Do not keep your doors closed,

my children. Open them to all and especially to those who are in need. Let your heart be a true source of love, peace, and sharing, my children. Think of those who suffer, and offer your prayers to God through his son, Jesus Christ, for his mercy we will each experience. God is love, my children; he values each of us. May others perceive the immense love that God has for us through you. May his spirit of love help you obtain the grace of holiness in your actions and your words. May the Virgin Mary, our mother, help you to pray; pray also to Jesus for all sinners, so that they experience God's mercy. Noël, Mum will always be among you. I did not abandon you, my children.

As much as I loved you on earth, I love you so much more in heaven. The love that we feel and send is unimaginable on earth. This love for you is incredible, improbable, and extraordinary. Everything around us is love. The love I feel and convey to you is deep, my children, and my messages are also signs of my love for you. I am with all of you, my children. I hear you when you speak to me. I see you when you speak to me. Your gestures of love are touching. Mum loves you more than you can imagine, my children. I am in you and around you without your knowledge. I am living among you. I love you, and I will always love you. Pray to God our Father through his son, Jesus. Pray to the Blessed Virgin Mary and all the saints and angels. Listen to those who talk to you in your heart. Mum loves you all.

—Gerda

Jesus loves you, my children. Follow him.

§§§

Spirit Writings: March 27, 2004; Start Time 8:30 p.m. End Time 9:30 p.m.

Me: Mum, it's I—Noël. Are you here?

Mum: Yes, Noël. It's I— Mum.

Me: Mum, it's so wonderful to meet with you.

Mum: Noël, I am with you forever. Mum will never leave you.

Me: Mum, guide us and send God, our Father, and his son, Jesus, our deep love.

Mum: Noël, my child, I always guide you. Love always the God of love and tenderness, in his son, Jesus. Your joy will be complete in the glory of God and his son.

Me: Mum, be happy. You deserve this new life full of happiness.

Mum: Noël, you might not understand the incredible happiness wherein I'm living. It is a wonderful life, Noël.

Me: I kiss you, Mum. Live your life near God, his son, and the heavenly assembly.

Mum: "I love you too. May peace be within all of my children.

Me: Mum, do you have any message for your children?

Mum: Love each other always, my children.

It is comforting for me to see you all united.

Love each other continuously. Live your life humbly and modestly. Always let peace be within you.

Mum is happy to see you be peacemakers, my children.

Follow Jesus forever. Mary leads you to him.

He talks to you; listen to him.

He is the salvation of the world.

Fast, my children, in these times.

Let the spirit of God guide you.

Pray, my children, for peace in families and in the world.

(I felt very strong pressure on my hand at this point.)

—Mum, Gerda

(The pressure on my hand grew stronger.)

Noël, this is really Mum.

Do you sense it? It is Mum, my Noële Aux Quatre Vents.

Mum sends you her love, all my children.

§§§

Remember that automatic/spirit writings is a physical phenomenon in mediumship; a spirit controls your spirit from the spirit world, and it is like you're in a trance. However, in my case, Mum takes control of me from the other side and guides me to write what she wants me to know. To do so, she communicates through my hand.

This particular message was quite intriguing, as when I felt the pressure of her hand over mine, it was as though Mum was proving to me again she was the true source of the messages. She warned me again not to doubt the source of the messages. Even though you want to believe, it is sometimes hard to continue trusting your own belief, especially when no one believes you. It is true that I was uncertain whether all these messages were from a higher frequency or dimension or if they were thoughts from my imagination.

Personal Prayer

"Lord Jesus, increase my faith. Help me to understand that in life, nothing is coincidence; all is God's will. Help me remember that you planned everything before we arrived, and there is a reason for everything. Moreover, help me to take a leap of faith every day, trusting that your grace is sufficient for me to do your will. Holy Spirit, Blessed Virgin Mary, and all the archangels, help me increase my faith. Amen."

Chapter 13

CELESTIAL THOUGHTS, MESSAGES, AND DREAMS

Spirit Writings: April 27, 2004; Start Time 4:00 a.m. End Time 4:43 a.m.

Me: Mum, are you here? I wish from this day you brought me what you want to bring me from beyond. At present, I am ready mum, ready to receive your gifts from heaven.

—Noël

I got the following response after waiting for five minutes.

Mum: Noël, finally, here you are!

Noël, my mission is to be a servant of God and to make you become one too. Let me shape you so that you will be an acceptable humble servant in the name of God. Noël, search for peace day and night. Serenity will then live in you. I will guide you to lift your soul to heaven. Enrich your soul with the

books you are reading. Listen only to the love that links with your heart. My heaven will become your heaven if you let me guide you. Go see the beauty of a sunrise. Our only God, who loves us infinitely, fills us with such endless beauty. Open your eyes to the rays of light. I love you, my daughter, and all of your siblings. I send you my full light.

Me: Thank you, Mum. Until tomorrow—take care.

Mum: I now leave, but I will be back, Noël. Take care of your body and your soul. I will be back soon.

§§§

It was remarkable that the first line she wrote was, "Noël … here you are!" It was as if she had been waiting for me for a while. In fact, I did not do any Spirit writing for a month. There was too much pressure from the family members who found the messages too "heavenly," or in other words, too "morbid". They warned me to let her rest in peace, considering that this practice was against our religion. My family also said that I should stop acting like a crazy woman. Therefore, I want to point out that those in the higher realms are waiting for us to communicate with them. They are there to help us, and they wait patiently for us to open the door to our mind. As we can't hear them, the only way to communicate with us is through our thoughts. Mum had patiently waited for me for a whole month to do Spirit writing. She desperately wanted me to be there. Therefore, after a whole month of silence, when I picked up my pen again, her reaction was very happy.

§§§

Spirit Writings: April 28, 2004; Start Time 1:48 a.m. End Time 2:38 a.m.

Me: Are you here, Mum? I am here ready to listen to you. I am true to our appointment for the union of our two souls with infinite love."

Mum: Noël, I'm glad you responded to my call. Wake up spontaneously and happy to hear me. You cannot find back lost time. Always be attentive and present for the heavenly call. God lives in you. Let your love attract you to him as endlessly as a magnet would. The dew on flowers lets the angels touch your soul. Thus, a flower does not dissociate with its perfume. Let heaven and the angels be an overflowing source of light for you all. All those who agree are inseparable. Noël, peace, humility, love, and faith must constantly live in each of you. Noël, watch the precious stones in nature. God fills you naturally too. Look no further. You are small and humble before him like an innocent child. If only you could guess how much God loves you.

Me: Mum, are you still happy?

Mum: I have never been happier, Noël. I found you. I found everyone through you.

Me: Mum, could you give me a message for Roberta,[51] who is very sad right now?

Mum: My poor one. She is ready to do anything to join me. Poor child, so fragile. Come back to me. I lost you. You were no longer near me. Do not play with fire. Be at peace with your soul, and be

---

[51] Fictitious name for sibling

serene. Tumult attracts tumults. Keep yourself from deviating on the wrong path. Instead, offer your sadness and suffering to God, so that he can transfigure them into wonderful things. Trust in God. Lift up your soul, and deny the pleasure of the flesh. Let the angels take care of you cheerfully. Shouldn't you be happy to accommodate them in your soul too? Be crazy for the Lord. Your folly should be for him only. I love you; do not lose the way anymore.

Me: Thanks, Mum. I will talk to you tomorrow. We love you.
Mum: I also love all of you. Bye for now.

Fall asleep peacefully, Noël. I will alert the angels.

§§§

Sometime later that same morning, I was outside my house. I had a fantastic view of the city and the harbor bay, as our house was uphill; I admired the splendour of the dawn, as Mum always reminded me to get energy from Mother Nature.

Suddenly a sentence came in my head like a dictation:

Inspirational Writing (Same Day); Start Time 6:00 a.m. End Time 6:07 a.m.

"Be like a flower waiting to bloom despite winds and storms."

I took my pencil and a sheet and wrote the following:

Be always a flower, just waiting to bloom despite winds and storms. Be like the endless beauty of a flower. May you always emanate supernatural fragrance like a flower's perfume. In your soul be like the beauty of a sunrise. Be as gentle as the touch from the sunshine.

§§§

Spirit Writings: April 29, 2004; Start Time 2:30 a.m. End Time 2:55 a.m.

Me: Hello, Mum, I am here. And you …?

Mum: Noël, I am present also, because I am the ladder you will climb to heaven. I am the bridge between you and God. I lead you to him.

Always pray to the Lord, because he really is the Lord in everything. Show him your love. Do not turn away from him. Accept your life, and be submissive. God has so many rewards for you. With the evil one, always be calm and at peace. The opposites of good and evil do not attract each other. Those who are not on your same frequency will eventually leave.

Nothing can harm you when the Spirit of God surrounds you.

Have no concerns, children. I am the rainbow.

Taste the beauty in paradise.

When I went to bed, I constantly had the following thought:

There are so many blessings in heaven;
Let the angels take care of you.

§§§

From the moment that I fell asleep that night, I dreamed of Mum. She had recovered from her illness and invited all of us home for a great meal together. In my dream, Malcom[52], a family member, raised a glass of whisky and made a toast to her recovery. However, Mum did not drink her glass of scotch. She wanted to party and told me "Noël, tomorrow and in the days that follow, we will Frolic." However, knowing that I had to go to work the next morning, I did not reply. Everyone was astonished to watch her excellent form and her amazing will to live after her terrible illness. In my subconscious, it was as if she had not died physically yet and wanted to party after her illness.

Then I had an extraordinarily vivid dream. I dreamed I was flying, or maybe I had an out-of-body experience. There was a slight breeze. The aerial view was amazing, and I flew like a bird. It was a beautiful dream; pigeons landed on me and let me caress them. The wind on my face, which refreshed me as I flew, gave me a feeling of infinite well-being. It was the most extraordinary dream I had in my entire life, apart from the beautiful one I had of the Virgin Mary. By using my hands like bird wings, I advanced slowly but surely. Really, it was an angelic dream—like a visit back home. I was blessed to have such a dream!

§§§

Same Day, Inspirational Writings: Start Time 5:55a.m. End Time 6:00 a.m.

---

[52] A sibling in my dream (Fictitious name)

Still dazzled by the dream in which I flew, I wrote the following thoughts:

The sky is wide open to you all. However, you cannot perceive it with your eyes. In dreams, anything is possible. Close your eyes more often to perceive angels. You will also see other unimaginable beauty. The dreams shatter the veil. Noël, I wish you celestial dreams.

§§§

Same Day, Inspirational Writings: Start Time 6:25 a.m. End Time 6:30 a.m.

On the road on my way to Mass, I received the following message. It was part of a conversation constantly going on in my mind.

The message said, **"Your life must be built heavenly. Work for heaven. An angel's smile, a loving eye, and a comforting word are all heavenly works."**

I noted it on a piece of paper before entering the church. I was now getting information not only through automatic/ spirit writings but also through my mind. I never thought back then that I was an inspirational-writing medium or practicing what we call mental mediumship. I did not know anything about mediumship back them. Receiving information from Mum this way was quite magic, but I was so amazed that I didn't think of asking myself how it was happening to me. I just embraced what I was getting.

§§§

Spirit Writings: April 30, 2004; Start Time 00:48 a.m. End Time 1:09 a.m.

Me: Mum?

Mum: Noël, thank you for coming faithfully, even though your body wants to sleep. This is how you should act. The desire of the mind must be stronger than the desire of the body. The body must dematerialise for the mind has space to act. Let your mind advise you and guide you always, and break the demanding desires from your body. Let the wisdom of the spirit take you further. Let the desires of the soul come first; the desires for the physical body come second.

Me: Thank you, Mum. Tell me more.

Mum: You fall asleep quickly; the angels are waiting for you. The celestial fairies will be there.

§§§

Same night 1:30 a.m. (before sleep)

In bed after my prayer and before immersing myself in sleep, many different voices sang to me. I would say it was a large crowd. The first time, a soprano, a tenor, or small children's voices (I heard two in solo) were singing. The second time, children and adult choirs sang together.

At least ten times, they sang, "Glory and Praise to you, Lord Jesus."

Was it the voice of angels waiting for me as Mum mentioned?

At 6:20 a.m. on my way to church, I received the following message in my mind:

Such is a new dawn, a possible renaissance for you. Do not hesitate to seize this new opportunity.

At 6:25 a.m. upon arrival to the church, I received another message through my thoughts.

Noël, where were you at the meeting of the angels? They were here, and you were not. Detach from human worries. Worry only about God the Father and works that you can do to please him.

§§§

Spirit Writings: May 1, 2004; Start Time 3:08 a.m. End Time 3:42 a.m.

Me: Mum, here I am. How are you? I love you, Mum. Despite the doubts of some members of our family, my faith remains intact in relation to our connection. However, it is hard for them to understand when they do not experience what I am living. I am sometimes sad about this misunderstanding and the lack of attention to your messages. Opinions differ, and each relative interprets our communication. Sometimes it hurts me bad to see and hear their reactions, because when they turn their back on me, it also hurts God and disgraces the gift he wants us to have. To him, we may seem insensitive, as if it does not affect us. Mum, I am hurt very badly because this path is so difficult for me, as it is so unthinkable for some to believe in the unseen. Guide them, Mum, while I do what I can.

Mum: Noël, do what you think is possible. Do everything, and accept anything from God. I will come in time and do what it takes to persuade those who still doubt our contacts. Noël, do not pay

attention to this slander. If people remained silent at times, they might not say things that hurt each other. Noël, continue to advance on your way to heaven. Let those who are still hesitant use their free will to believe or not. It is not for us to judge them. Otherwise, Noël, I learn more in heaven. This is wonderful. I am illuminated.

I have learned so much since my arrival here, Noël. I would like you to see all this. It is so beautiful. Do not let others influence you, Noël, in regards to our contact.

The truth is in your heart.

What you feel is real. Now, go back to sleep.

As the wind blows, let the Spirit of God be the breath of life for you.

§§§

Spirit Writings: May 2, 2004; Start Time 2:10 a.m. End Time 2:20 a.m.

Me: Are you here? I am home.[53]

Mum: Noël, here I am. I love our meetings. It is good that you came. I see you are tired, so I will not be long. It makes me happy to see you in my home. I like to be there. Noël, even though I am happy here, sometimes I miss you all. I want us to all meet again one day; I am here at present, but for you all to see me again, you have to cross the veil. However, the time will come when God calls you back to him. I love

---

[53] Mum's house

you, my children. Do not think I forgot you. I didn't in my earthly life, and I will not in my heavenly life. You are part of me.

Those who remain united, my children, will never disunite.

§§§

Spirit Writings: May 3, 2004; Start Time 2:33 a.m. End Time 3:13 a.m.

Me: Mum, you know my state of mind in relation to what has happened with Ben.[54] I am still in a state of shock, and I cannot digest how someone could have tried to cause his physical death. Was it voluntary or involuntary? I am worried for him, Mum. You know how I am. It was as if they hated me too, and I'm really disgusted by what happened.

A colleague of Ben offered him a piece of cake without telling him that there was a high dose of drugs in it. Ben had never touched drugs in his life, so he found himself in the emergency unit, where they busily worked to save his life. Because of a piece of cake, he faced death and could have left his wife and son behind. Maybe the colleague did not think he would react so badly to drugs, but if it was a joke, it was of a very bad nature. Alternatively, could the colleague have done it intentionally to harm him? We will never know, as Ben resigned from his position sometime

---

[54] Fictitious name for sibling

after this incident. I guess he would never have been able to trust these people again.

Mum: Noël, do not forget that evil is gaining ground on earth. In addition, wickedness abounds in people's souls. What happened to Ben was the worst sort of evil action that one could do to a friend. Ben actually has no sincere friends around him. Beware, children. So many evil people surround you, and we have trouble hunting them down, especially when they come in force. We have lost so many souls this way. That is why I ask you to pray always for protection. Noël, life is full of pitfalls. Move away from the forces of evil, and help Ben to the extent that it is possible. He needs all your help and support. He is discouraged. Ben, I pray for you. Approach my ray of light; it will protect you from negative waves. Do not approach dark waves anymore. I care for you, and I want you to be happier. Noël, join our prayers to overcome evil. Stay far away from all negativity and evil activities. There are so many unhealthy things, my children, and nobody is safe unless he or she is prepared. Noël, let us pray together so that we gain more and more souls for God, our Father. I love you, my children, and I want you near me, but you must do your mission before joining me. Pray for God to preserve you from the clutches of evil. Always be on your guard towards everyone you approach who is bad in the soul. Bye. Stay under my ray of light.

§§§

Spirit Writings: May 4, 2004; Start Time 5:50 a.m. End Time 6:00 a.m.

Me: Mum, we all love you.

Mum: Noël, I love you all. Love God through his son a hundred times more than you love me. Your love for the Son and the Father should have no boundaries. Love each other limitlessly. I love you limitlessly as well. May a new sun bring new warmth in your heart.

§§§

Spirit Writings: May 5, 2004; Start Time 5:16 a.m. End Time 5:29 a.m.

Mum: Noël, good morning to you and to my children, grandchildren, and great-grandchildren.
The peace of the Lord is with you. The sky overflows with graces that are waiting for someone to choose them. Let the angels come to you and help you daily. Be constantly in a state of grace. God expects so much of you. Give him your fruit. Always follow the path leading to God, the Redeemer. Let your life be a road, paved with flowers of the sweetest scents. Let your heart respond to the call in the silence. Pray, meditate, and improve yourselves, my children, to save lost souls.

§§§

Spirit Writings: 6 May 2004; Start Time 5:07 a.m. End Time 5:17 a.m.

Mum: Let us take care of you today. The angels wait for that [for us to request their help].

You seem tired. I will leave you. See you soon, my daughter. Continue your celestial work on earth. I love you all. You and I are one.

§§§

Mum was right. I was exhausted from sleepless nights. I was up most nights to be present for the messages. However, little by little, fatigue slowed me in my daily routine. I had two children to look after and full-time work. So yes, I really was tired. Even though I was exhausted, I would not give up or ignore the magic I was experiencing.

Same Day through thoughts in my mind:

Inspirational Writings: Start Time 6:02 a.m. End Time 6:05 a.m.

Be pure to join us.
Prepare to join us.
Purify your soul, your spirit.
For similar souls, interact.
Efforts it takes to get to us.
Begin to reject pleasures
Which confuse your mind.
In addition, prevent you from seeing the wonders of God.
God gave you a body and a holy spirit.
Do not mutilate them.

§§§

Spirit Writings: May 10, 2004; Start Time 5:06 a.m. End Time 5:43 a.m.

Me: Mum, I am here. Are you nearby as well? Do you have a message for us today? Love you and always will, Mum.

Mum: Noël and my other children, I love you all deeply. Do not be sad when thinking of me.

Me: Mum, your children sometimes do not understand your messages, and interpretations sometimes play on their minds. I am a little disheartened to read your messages to them sometimes. However, you are bound to them too, so I make them read the messages and convey all your thoughts but again, they do not always understand the contents as you would. We are not from your level, Mum. Can you send us messages that are easy to understand? We are so far from you. Thank you, Mum.

Mum's messages were becoming too clever for us to understand. It was as if we could no longer follow her level of wisdom. Moreover, we felt lost, as this new language of mum shocked us. She seemed to be so different. It seemed she was at a much higher level of awareness or a higher dimension wherein her knowledge of things, words, wisdom, action, guidance, and inspiration grew beyond our human level.

Mum: Yes, Noël, but my messages are still so easy to understand. If I convey more things, you will not understand anything.

I think that Mum wanted us to understand that if she told us or could tell us more things, we would be completely lost, as it would be beyond what we could comprehend.

Me: Is it vast, Mum, where you are? What about the knowledge?

Mum: Noël, it is vast and infinite. As we ascend, knowledge increases.

Me: Mum, what do you look like now?

Mum: I am no longer like the person that left you. My being is light.

Me: Have you friends around you? Do you have any work to do?

Mum: Yes, I do have friends. We work all the time at different missions.

Me: Which ones?

Mum: Some are on earth; others are in heaven.

Me: And God, is he near you?

Mum: We feel his presence everywhere. There is a long way to reach his kingdom. Everything is done for God, our Father, through his son, Jesus.

Me: Thank you, Mum, for responding to my questions. We embrace you tightly. We all send you our eternal love.

Mum: Thank you, Noël. You are also in my heart eternally.

§§§

Spirit Writings: May 11, 2004; Start Time 5:02 a.m. End Time 5:21 a.m.

Me: My being of light, our protector from heaven: kisses and love from all of us your children, grandchildren and great-grandchildren. Always be happy, Mum.

Mum: Noël, thank you for sending me all these wishes of love. I am deeply touched. You stay written on my heart. God has infinite love for each of us created in his image. Love him more than anyone else. His son also has infinite love for each of us. Love him, and wish for him in your heart. The angels from heaven are here to lead you to them. Let the magic of the angels of light guide you.

§§§

Spirit Writings: May 12, 2004; Start Time 5:24 a.m. End Time 5:40 a.m.

Me: Mum conveys my eternal love to God and his son on this day. Our family is always under his heavenly protection.

This thought came to my mind just before the next message:

"Pray, Noël, and the blessings will fall from heaven like mana.[55]"

Mum: Noël, thank you for being here. Pray for the others, Noël, always. We hear all your prayers. Do not stop talking to angels as you talk to me and to God and his son, Jesus. Angels are waiting to help you. Also, pray to the saints, Noël. Pray to Jesus, and pray to Mary. Pray sincerely, and listen in silence. I am protecting you.

—Mum

---

[55] Bread

Me: We miss you, Mum.

§§§

Spirit Writings: May 13, 2004; Start Time 7:15 a.m. End Time 7:30 a.m.

Me: Mum, I wanted to apologize to you. I went back to sleep this morning and could not be faithful to our meeting. Despite this, Mum, know that you are always in my heart and the hearts of all your children. You are unforgettable, Mum, and the love that we have for you exceeds all mysteries.

I received the following after five minutes. I almost thought that I would have to answer, as the wait was long.

Mum: Noël, love goes beyond the imagination. Always be attentive to our call. Peace and love be in you all on this day. Noël, be faithful to our meetings.
Do not miss an inner call. I will send you a shower of roses. Continue to pray, Noël. I am close to you all. Go where I lead you, and stay in my light. Pray to the Virgin Mary, Noël. Request her always.
Me: Thanks for answering, Mum.

§§§

Spirit Writings: May 14, 2004; Start Time 4:35 a.m. End Time 5:15 a.m.

Me: Hello, dear Mum. I want to convey the feelings of respect from each of your children. We all love you and always keep you in our hearts. This morning, I am sending you special love from Lily,[56] who carries you in her heart. She wants a little message from you this morning for herself and her family.

Mum: Thank you, Noël, for always remembering me with your love. You will never be separated from my heart. Dear one, my child, thank you for keeping me at the bottom of your heart. Be strong. We will meet you. Disconnect from all inner torment and fear. Confide your fears in Mary. Request and pray.

God saves those who believe. Without faith, you will face judgment. Have courage. There are so many angels around your family. Pray for heavenly protection on each of you. The road will be difficult. However, put all your trust in God. I send you my blessing, my child. Moreover, your little angel realized miracles for your family like a diamond in the sky. Pray, pray, pray for support. Noël, convey to all my children that I love them. Moreover, they are always in me and could not be anywhere else.

Always love, my children,

In your words,

Your actions,

Your looks,

Your listening,

Your smile.

And holding hands.

May divine love always reflect through you.

Bye, Noël, for now. I am glad you came to our meeting. Always stay in wakefulness.

---

[56] Nickname to protect identity

§§§

Spirit Writings: May 15, 2004; Start Time 6:02 a.m. End Time 6:15 a.m.

Mum: Noël and all my children, may you be blessed. As a wave crashes on a rock, I fall on you all. I throw myself into your soul to guide you. Rise up, dear children and grandchildren of my heart. Work for God.
Peace and love always.
Be sincere. Be just.
Be wise.
Be the sweet scents of flowers.

§§§

Spirit Writings: May 16, 2004; Start Time 6:06 a.m. End Time 6:22 a.m.

Me: Hello, Mum. Good day! Can you please help Mr James[57] make an important decision? Request that the angels send him their light. I send you again our undying, endless love, Mum.
Mum: Despite your deep sleep and half-awake state, you answered, Noël. Always put the desires of the soul first. Noël, thank you for your effort. I send you all my light. You will see beyond all things. Entrust everything to your Father, the God of the visible and invisible universe.

57　Family friend

Do not worry for Mr James; we lights will surround him as he makes his decision. I only want your happiness. However, do not forget to give yourself fully to God and his son. I send all my love through the veil to reach each of you in your heart. Love yourself as God loves you. I intensely love you, my grandchildren, great-grandchildren, and children. I bless you all.

§§§

Spirit Writings: May 17, 2004; Start Time 4:42 a.m. End Time 4:49 a.m.

Me: Mum, are you here? We remain under your light, Mum.
Mum: Noël, I am always here. I look forward to all of you always.
Me: We all kiss you, Mum. Be happy.

§§§

Spirit Writings: May 18, 2004; Start Time 4:56 a.m. End Tine 5:21 a.m.

Me: Mum, I am here, listening.
Mum: Noël.
Me: Do you have anything special to say to me, Mum?
Mum: Saying your name is already a lot, don't you think?
Me: Yes, Mum, you are so right. Seeing you write my name on paper is the most beautiful treasure that you could offer me at this time.

Mum: I know this month reminds you of my last moments with you.

Do not be sad.

Do not have any regrets.

I have everything I desire.

I'm so happy, my children.

Look ahead, never backwards.

Me: Mum, we all convey our love to Mary, our heavenly mother, this month.

Mum: Mary loves you so much. She is a mother to all. Entrust all your troubles to her always. She is wonderful and inexplicably beautiful. Pray to her always. Thank her for all her blessings as well as her son, Jesus, lamb of God and saviour of the world.

Always love Jesus, my children.

Follow him with blind faith.

Me: Mum, we love you.

Mum: I love you.

We are not separate as night is not separate from the day.

As the night becomes the day and the day becomes the night, I am equally attached to you.

However, I do not know how long I will be permitted to write you.

Me: Mum, the important thing is that you are happy.

Mum: Yes, Noël, I am.

My life is a very happy one.

I live wonderfully.

Me: I kiss you again, and so do all my siblings.

§§§

Spirit Writings: May 19, 2004; Start Time 4:56 a.m. End Time 5:13 a.m.

Me: Hello, Mum. I am here. You are always in our hearts, Mum. Send us your light always. Thank you, Mum, for helping us constantly. Convey our love to all those who help us in heaven.

—Noël

Mum: Take care, all of my children;
> **God cares about his children;**
> **He loves you all;**
> **Those who perform the work of our Lord**
> **Do well always;**
> **Make peace;**
> **Make love every day.**
> **Share the love;**
> **Be love always.**
> **Turn your eyes to the sky;**
> **Crave him.**
> **This is your source of living water, my children;**
> **Your eyes should always be towards the sky; do not forget.**

§§§

Spirit Writings: May 20, 2004; Start Time 6:05 a.m. End Time 5:13 a.m.

Me: Mum, Chris[58] will experience a great change in his life today. He will be fixed on his future.

---

[58] Family member

Mum: May Chris follow the outlined path. A bright future awaits him, a much better one. He can go without fear. His family will join him soon. Trust the doors that open before you unexpectedly. Among us, there are those who influence people on earth to bring them to you. Always be confident in the strength and power of the angels. Put your trust fully in God our Father. Chris walks in pure confidence now; he follows easily guidance.

Me: Thanks, Mum, for your message. Live your new life fully. Kisses,

—Noël

§§§

Spirit Writings: May 21, 2004; Start Time 5:04 a.m. End Time 5:35 a.m.

Me: Mum, it has been a year already since the day you entered the hospital. Nobody would have thought that we would lose you eight days later. You suffered so much, Mum, but now you are at peace. A year ago, we learned the sad truth, but everything is always in our hearts as if it was yesterday. We love you so much, Mum.

Mum: Noël, sadness is in your heart and mine too, because you are my children. Losing you all hurt me, and sometimes it is still painful, despite my new life. However, if grief saddens you so, offer it to our Lord. Your heart is heavy with sorrow, and you send me your state of mind. Have courage; God is present. He loves you and helps you. I am also sad because I cannot talk to you, and you cannot hear me. Think

of all those who are suffering similar losses. You have the opportunity to read my words, and they do not have any consolation. You must share everything I am telling you, so they find comfort, peace, and hope. I leave you for now, Noël. There is too much sadness around you. Try to be happy for me. I love you. I have not forgotten you. You were in me when I left the earth—in my arms and in my heart. You suffer because your love for me is intact. Nobody can take this from you, not even the passage of time. God understands your suffering; give it to him, the Almighty God. He will fill you with grace. I love you all, and I'm with you all.

§§§

Spirit Writings: June 1, 2004; Start Time 4:05 a.m. End Time 5:35 a.m.

Me: My dear mum, the difficult times in memory of the one-year anniversary of your departure are over, fortunately. It was a difficult week and sad weekend for us all. We miss you so much, Mum. We all want to see you again and hold you in our arms. We love you so much. It has been a year already, but we have not forgotten you. You remain in our hearts. You were the centre of our reunion, and we felt your physical absence at home. It is very hard sometimes to see everything the way you left it. Despite our heavy sorrow, be happy where you are.

Mum: I love you. Live your lives, my children. Look straight ahead. Life has mysteries that you do not know. If you only knew, you would not be sad for me. Live for God, my children; reap the benefits of heaven. In this difficult time for you, pray that a dove descends on you, my children. I am always with you. Nothing separates us, my children and grandchildren—nothing.

—Mum

§§§

Spirit Writings: June 2, 2004; Start Time 5:00 a.m. End Time 5:20 a.m.

Mum: I am here; Mum is here.

Life has difficult moments and moments of intense joy.

Enjoy every moment, because everything must be accomplished

In the Lord and never without the Lord.

May the Lord be with you always.

Wherever you go,

In whatever you do,

Bless the Lord forever;

Give him eternal glory.

Do not cling to the things of the earth;

Work for heaven and the Lord;

God must be the centre of your life, children—

The Father, Son, and Holy Spirit in oneness,

Three in one.

Our Lord, king of heaven and earth,

To him be power and glory everlasting.

§§§

Spirit Writings: June 3, 2004; Start Time 5:00 a.m. End Time 5:30 a.m.

Me: Mum, Emilie[59] as well as Aurelie[60] would like a little message from you if you want this.

Mum: Emilie, my dear, it takes courage, and you will need more of it, but never be desperate. Offer God your suffering. Never lose faith in him. Never turn aside from following him. I see your pain, and I know how your mother's heart bleeds. Keep your faith and pray to God. You will find true joy in him. He loves you endlessly. Turn to him and his infinite love. Do not persist in hitting doors that will never open. Rather, look for relief close to God, the one who offers you his eternal love.

My Aurelie,
Push your boat right to the front; do not stop at the first incident. The wind continues to blow on the sails. Like a boat gliding on the water, we blow on you and help you move forward. We grow and find strength through tests. One day, whatever is reserved for you will come to you. Have faith, and smile at life. I love you. Have courage.

§§§

What mum said to Aurelie was so right, as she went through a horrible experience with someone whom she

---

[59] Sibling (Fictitious name)
[60] Emilie's daughter (Fictitious name)

155

had thought deeply loved her. A couple of months after Mum's message, Aurelie met a good-hearted man who flew from Europe just to meet her. They fell in love at first sight. They were engaged and then got married just before Emilie (Aurelie's mum) passed over. God offered Emilie the opportunity to assist in her daughter's wedding and to see where Aurelie lived overseas before she passed away unexpectedly in Aurelie's arms. I had no doubt that Mum was waiting for her on the other side, smiling at her and embracing her. I always loved Emilie; she was my dearest friend; she always enjoyed Mum's messages, and I was very close to her. Moreover she was my godmother.

§§§

Spirit Writings: June 4, 2004; Start Time 5:25 a.m. End Time 5:35 a.m.

Mum: Follow the angels where they lead you.
By following them, let the will of the Lord be done.

§§§

Spirit Writings: June 7, 2004; Start Time 4:50 a.m. End Time 5:16 a.m.

Me: Mum, Nicolas[61] joined Pascaline[62] overseas today. It's amazing, Mum. Thank God for the wonders he accomplishes for us and in us.

---

[61] Family member
[62] Family member

Mum: Superabundant joy and a fantastic reunion were present today. God reunites those who love each other. There is happiness when brotherly love exists. God allows it; he decides our lives, my children. Moreover, the will of the Lord is fulfilled through the intercession of angels. Our Lord does wonders in all things and all places. Glory to him eternally. I am very proud of my Nicolas; a new beginning awaits him. Bless the Lord, my children. Praise him forever. Nicolas, my child, your efforts will be rewarded. Go further, Nicolas. Follow the outlined path. Surpass yourself, my child. Raise yourself. Your son will be very proud of you one day. I love you eternally, my children. Pray and thank God for all the gifts.

—Mum

§§§

Mum said, "Follow the outlined path." Today, I can clearly see the path that really was outlined as Nicolas followed Mum's advice and followed his intuition and proper guidance. It is amazing indeed how his life changed 100 per cent for the better.

§§§

Spirit Writings: June 8, 2004; Start Time 4:56 a.m. End Time 5:06 a.m.

Planetary Event: Venus passed in front of the sun.

Mum: A planetary phenomenon brings many changes in your life. Be ready to receive its benefits. Make sure of the time, and desire positive changes in your heart. This day is very important, my children. This is an event but also a sign. Good day!

§§§

Spirit Writings: June 9, 2004; Start Time 4:56 a.m. End Time 5:29 a.m.

Mum: You must sincerely offer to God what you sow and harvest. Every action and word towards our Lord must be in relation to love. Love God without limits. This is your motto on earth.

§§§

Spirit Writings: June 11, 2004; Start Time 3:51 a.m. End Time 4:23 a.m.

Me: Mum, I just saw you in my dreams. It is a magical moment when I get to sleep and see you alive and real in a dream. Dreaming of you is magic because I see you again, and everything seems natural and precise. Mum, help us in our daily lives. I love you so much, Mum, and all your beautiful children. Life happens, and we don't forget anything. Your mark in our lives is still intact. Mum, do I have a mission to accomplish with all these messages? Give me an answer soon if you do not mind. I am ready for all the desires of the heavenly angelic beings that are bonded as a whole with God, his son, and the Holy Spirit.

Mum: Noël, my child, peace be with you always. Heaven is magical, Noël. Do not forget that so many things are possible to us here. You have to try to elevate yourself, and you will be rewarded. You will discover the fairy magic of heaven. Continue your path with determination, and think about giving more of yourself. You will know where we want to see you arrive. Detach yourself from bodily desires, and target the mysteries of heaven and its assembly around our one and only God, our Lord who made heaven and earth in its entirety.

My child, go further. Discover what is good and true forever.

Have courage; I am with you every moment. Have Jesus on your lips always, my children and grandchildren.

Bye for now, Noël.

§§§

Spirit Writings: June 14, 2004; Start Time 5:38 a.m. End Time 6:02 a.m.

Me: Mum, I'm still very upset by the film The Passion of the Christ. *In principle, films are far from being real, so we tell ourselves that it cannot have happened that way. However, what if it really did? When we reflect on the movie, we say to ourselves, "If Jesus suffered all these atrocities, it becomes so painful to bear". His passion was more than a nightmare, and the price he had to pay for the redemption of our sins is undoubtedly high. I'm still very sad that we could have tortured the Christ like that; it is so inhuman.*

Mum: Jesus, the king of the universe forever, is in your hearts;
Without him in your life, you have no eternal life;
His passion testifies about his immeasurable love
For us, friends and enemies;
Jesus's eternal love and sacred heart with a thousand lights;
Wounds in loving hands, warmly ...
Nailed feet, warmth, and softness of his steps;
Living Jesus, glorious on the right of the Father;
Jesus, I love you;
Repeat these words:
I need you and I love you, Jesus, today, until the last days, and eternally.
Love you, Jesus, eternally.

§§§

Spirit Writings: June 18, 2004; Start Time 4:52 a.m. End Time 5:16 a.m.

Me: Mum, I hope you are always well and that you become increasingly brighter. In exactly one week, Mum, we will live a very great moment in the family: a wedding scheduled for next Friday. These two quite surprised us by saying yes to each other, but if this is the will of God, it will be done without protest. Everything about him is wonderful.
Mum: Noël, do not be so sad like that;
Never lose faith in a better life;
God provides his children with everything;
God works in us, and the results are the fruits,
The work God does in us.

God loves you, my children;
Show him, too, your love.
I am happy;
Today, my life has a meaning.
Show charity and humility always, my children;
Be humbled by our Lord.
I send my blessing to both.
May they live their sacrament in goodness and truth
With holiness.

§§§

Spirit Writings: July 7, 2004; Start Time 3:20 a.m. End Time 3:40 a.m.

Mum: My **Noële Aux Quatre Vents**, I know about your resentment. Do not lose your great faith. In addition, give this inner suffering as an offering to our Lord. You fight hard, and we all know that.

The road is rough and difficult. You will have to be patient. Always take care of your children. Do not flee from your responsibilities regarding them. I protect your children in my light. Noël, before, you would never dare do certain things. Fill your life with love, Noël. Moreover, do not let any lower resentment invade you.

I will always be near you. I will help you; be certain. Noël, never cease your prayers to find the light. Pray endlessly with faith. Have courage; I am near you.

—Mum

Mum evidently knew the tribulations I was going through. This was the last message I wrote to Mum in 2004, [two years after the first message] as I was facing many issues in my personal life. Nothing was working in my marriage, at work, or in my life in general. I was tired of everything. In addition, I was falling deeper and deeper into a severe depressive state. I had so much weighing me down since Mum's death a year earlier, and then my close relative Paul's illness took place, and my personal life was a real dilemma; I was facing emptiness and unhappiness. I was completely lost.

Chapter 14

MOVING TO VICTORIA

I needed to go away. I was falling apart. Therefore, I decided to go on holiday to Australia in December 2004. This trip opened up a new life for my family and me. I trusted my instincts against my siblings' advice, and I went alone. I had to do it. I felt compelled to go and leave everything and everyone behind. "This is not something to do", my family said to me. However, I was right. I spent five weeks there at the Balancy's family: deep thanks to my cousin Medou for having me and decided to return to Australia permanently when I came back home. I had had enough of the place where I was living and enough of my marriage feeling unhappy. I had experienced enough of the overpopulated island, enough of the corrupted politicians, and enough of people's racist treatment towards each other in my homeland. There was no future for my two children there. In addition, I had had enough of my full-time job for the same private company for seventeen years and the disrespect between the communities and the dangerous things that were happening—robberies, crimes, and insecurity all over the island. I was very upset when a thief smashed my car door and stole my brand new CD player that I bought at the duty-free shop when I came back from Australia. I wanted a safer life for my two beautiful children. That was my priority. I didn't matter, my marriage didn't matter, and my husband didn't matter; I was focused on getting my children out of that environment specially where I was living. I appreciated Australia, as I experienced the difference when I went there. In my homeland, my bosses wanted me to call them sir, madam, mister, and so forth. I could never call them by their first name. In Australia, everyone went by his or her first name. In French-speaking terms, I was expected to address my boss by the *vous* form and never *tu*. The latter was so disrespectful in Mauritius. I submitted my resignation letter a couple months after my return from Australia as soon as I obtained my visa. I have never been happier in my entire life than that day, as I knew a new life was about to start for my children and myself. Today, when I think about some of my past bosses, especially one of them who hurt my self-esteem deeply I smile as I remember how vulnerable I was back then and how strong of a woman I am today. I wouldn't let anyone hurt me today the way he did back then. I am sending you blessings, wherever you are, and I free myself from any resentment towards you, dear. I found peace, and I hope you will find it too. You know who you are and if not God will remind you that one day at your return to the source. We are all beautiful souls and children of God, made in his image, and no one has the right to treat us badly. Do not ever let anyone make you feel little. I will never let this happen again, as I am a divine soul.

§§§

I flew to Australia with my daughter at the end of June 2005. I was there on a student visa, studying full-time. The challenges were difficult for me, but the only thing that mattered was providing my two children with a better life and better opportunities in a much bigger country. I unfortunately had to leave my son Loïc behind, as I wanted to find a place for all of us. Furthermore, the family housing us only had room for two of us. I was heartbroken to leave him with his dad, but I had no choice. I faced severe depression, as the adaptation was hard. Being on holiday and residing in the country was completely different. Moreover, I did not have much help. Therefore, we stayed with my ex-husband's work colleague Henriette for two weeks. I had never met her before, so it was essentially a complete stranger's house. However, she made us feel very comfortable; she was such a lovely woman who welcomed us into her sweet little home. It was winter, and I remember talking to my sister Marie Josée (who would pass over only two months later) on the phone under the blanket. I was crying, as I was already facing depression and anxiety about the future after recently arriving in Australia. I was in a country that I did not know much about, living at a stranger's place, with no one to count on but myself while dealing with the aforementioned challenges. Six months earlier, there were parties. Six months later, I faced the very hard reality of adjusting to the culture, the climate, and the cost of everything. Miraculously, after only two weeks, my house rental application was approved and my daughter and I moved in there safely. I felt so happy and uplifted again. Where there was a will, there was a way. I needed to fight, and I was fighting on my own. My son could have joined us then, but my ex-husband waited three more months to join us because of his work in our homeland. Life was not easy for me. I was on my own, fighting for survival as an international student and paying for the courses, more than $25,000 over a period of two years. The rent wasn't cheap either, at $1,000 monthly and there were utilities to pay: gas, electricity, water, telephone, food, clothes, and school uniforms. My children could only go to private school, and I had to pay the tuition monthly as well as aftercare. On top of that, the terms of the student visa didn't allow me to work more than twenty hours per week. I cannot tell you what I went through to make ends meet.

To add to my depression, two months after my arrival in Australia, I received a phone call announcing that my eldest sister, Marie Josée,[63] had passed away while on holiday in Monaco, France. This was a terrible shock. The last time we said goodbye to each other when she dropped me at the airport in Mauritius, I didn't know I would never see her again on earth. The world was crumbling at my feet. Because of my depression, I lost twenty kilograms. I was becoming more fragile, as I was only forty-nine kilograms. It was hard to adapt quickly to the spoken language, the cold weather, and the new culture; it was also difficult to sit back in your late thirties and hear that you do not know administration duties. I had to cope with it, despite my years in an office doing administrative and accounting duties for fifteen years full time in my homeland. On top of that, I needed to work night shifts. I took everything: packing, cleaning, catering, data entry, customer service,

---

[63]   Marie Josée, my eldest sister

service cashier, office cashier, administrative officer, and so forth. I did not have any excuses for not adapting, as this was my chance to succeed away from my homeland. We had invested so much money in this project that I could not fail; I was the primary applicant for the permanent residency, and this move was my sole idea. My soon-to-be ex-husband finally arrived with my son four months after my daughter and I did, in October 2005. I was so happy to hug my little boy again at Melbourne Airport. Tears of joy rolled down my cheeks. I realized how much he must have missed me while living with his dad for several months. He came back to me with anxiety causing a moderate stutter by the stress he had endured from not seeing his mum and sister at home the day Caroline and I left. I cried that day when I left him at school, knowing I would not see him that afternoon [as well as my three lovely dogs, Gypsy, Reine, and Duc]. This was the ever hardest day of my whole entire life. My daughter and I were on the plane to Australia. All this was heartbreaking. Leaving everything behind was not easy, but I never looked back. It was a heavy decision, but I made it, as I trusted my instinct. Everything is going to be all right, my son; you will see. I will never leave you again. Loïc and Caroline, you are my reason for living and fighting so hard. I love you both endlessly. My soon-to-be ex-husband left me again two months later, this time alone with both children, in December 2005. He travelled between Australia and our homeland two more times for work and personal matters. He had difficulty adapting himself to everything here: the language barrier, the weather, and, more importantly, work itself. I would not give up. I kept pulling my head out of the water. "I will not drown", I promised myself. Life was a nightmare, but I kept my chin up and worked extreme hours, seven days and seven nights a week, to survive and to give my children what they needed for their education and pushing hard to obtain our permanent residency. I refused to go back to where I was staying in my homeland. "I will not go back to that life", I said to myself. Mum and I could not be wrong. No, I had to fight, so I did. I catered Christmas lunch as a chef at someone's house. This family was celebrating the holiday, and my heart felt sorrowful, as I was just a worker to them. Tears fell from my eyes as I thought about my two children who were home on their own, waiting for me to come back on Christmas Day. Moreover, I had no presents to give them, as we severely lacked money. My heart was deeply hurt. I will never forget how hard Christmas 2005 was. I remember all shops were closed contrary to our homeland and I had to look for some little presents at the supermarket for them after my work.

In addition to work, I was studying full-time for two consecutive years with almost no sleep, as I had many projects, reports, and homework assignments. I finally succeeded in all my courses after twenty-four months of hard work. I applied for permanent residency, which I obtained successfully for my two children, their dad and myself in February 2008. I was relieved that I had survived on my own for two years in a new country, renting my own house with my two children. It was very hard, but I was proud that I had done it. My life was tough. I can't tell you all I've been through to get where I am today, as it's too painful to go into detail with everything. Sometimes, bad things are better to keep private, as it's too painful to talk about them or even remember them.

Chapter 15

MESSAGES FROM FRANC MEDIUM AND SISTER MAJO

I have not tried automatic/spirit writings for three years. I had to deal with problems as well as the move to Australia; the passing over of my sister Marie Josée; and my depressive state, panic attacks, and anxiety from making ends meet. Moreover, I dealt with all the stress of going to school and then going to work in the evening or over the weekend. Life was tough for me. I tried communicating with Mum again around the time I had a phone call from my sister Monique, in France, who told me that a medium called Franc wanted to talk to me about Mum and that he had a message for me. He woke me up at five in the morning to pass me the message in my ears that Mum wanted me to start automatic/ spirit writings again.

Spirit Writings: September 2, 2007; Start Time 7:00 a.m. End Time 7:20 a.m.

I wrote the following message after the phone call with Franc, the medium from Paris:

Me: Mum, thank you for coming to me. I am sorry I cut off contact with you. I did not listen to my heart, and the words that made me doubt our communication influenced me. I know you are not upset with me, Mum. I am very weak, and I feel doubt again. Please forgive me. I know you already have forgiven me or you do not have to, as you love me. I am again at your disposal, Mum. Tell me what you need to convey to the family. I love you. Thank you for your words just now, Mum, through this medium Franc de Paris[64]. Thank you for being there for all of us whom you love. I am waiting mother. I love you.

Mum: Mum is with you all. I love you always and eternally.

Mum is here to help you through the painful steps.

I am constantly with each of you.

You are my children, and I, your mother, will always be there for you. Stay strong and have courage. I am among you.

It may seem incredible, but I am always with each of you. I advise you and guide you. Receive my calls. Do not close your ears. Do not be afraid of what you think is impossible, unthinkable, or unimaginable. Do not go towards discouragement or depression. Nothing makes me sadder than when I see you lost. I am here to help you. I love you. Pray always. God always helps you because he loves you. I am happy to talk to you again. Thank you for allowing me to do

---

64   French Medium, friend of my sister Monique

so. Do not be sad. Be happy like lights twinkling in an eternal space. Be at peace in your mind. Open up and welcome the unimaginable. Mum loves you all. I am happy, and Majo[65] is with me. She also loves you and embraces you. She is happy at last. She has no regrets. She guides you. Noël, thank you for doubting no longer.

This is I, your mum, who chose you to be the spokesperson, the messenger.

You will see what happens now. Do you still doubt? I am here and alive; I never died. Do not weep for us. We are happy. You will understand one day the wonders of where we are and why we do not regret anything. We are here to help those who need light. My children, I love you, and I hold you in wakefulness. I will come to talk to you and see you. I am eternal. Do not blame yourself for my departure. I am happy. Be equally happy. Tell Del[66] that Majo sends her kisses, love, and protection.

My children, I protect you too. I love you.

I hear you and receive you; receive me also when I call you or talk to you. Open your heart to me, your mother, who never stops loving you. I will always love you. I stay close to all of you and protect you always.

Noël, remain awake. I will come back. Stay attentive to the call of the beyond.

---

[65] Nick name for my eldest sister Marie-Josée who passed over unexpectedly in Sep 2005.

[66] Del is Majo's daughter

**I love you. I embrace you. Stay strong. You have
strength that I give you. Otherwise, you would have
taken another path.**
I love you.

—Mum

§§§

Spirit Writings: September 4, 2007; Start Time 10:08 p.m.
End Time 11:16 p.m.

*Me: Hi, Mum, and hi, Majo. I am sending you our love and
tender kisses. We love you. We never forget either of you.
You remain in our hearts. Our love goes through space and
travels in your direction. Nothing is between us, especially
not the fact that we cannot see you or hear you. You are
still present. We feel you, and we know it. Thank you for
your support and love. It makes us believe the impossible is
possible. Our eyes and ears are still closed. For you, all is
clear. For us, it is not yet. However, little by little, we are
able to follow you and go beyond what is really happening.
We are happy for you, to be sure. We love you. We wait for
you. You and all those with you that we hold so dear are
always welcome. Send them our eternal love too.*
*Majo, we think strongly of you today. It has been two years
since your spirit left your body and went to heaven. You
are light now, and I am glad you are finally serene and
happy. I love you. Your children love you. Viv[67] loves you*

---

[67]   Majo's husband Nickname for Vivian

too. I know you are with them now, even as Del[68] and Viv are on your journey.

You are with them. You are happy to see them together. You are proud that they are honouring you by this pilgrimage. You pray for them. You are happy about their journey. Mum and Majo, if you wish to send us a message to the family, do it. I am at your disposal. I kiss you, and I love you so much.

—Noëlette

The letter *M* now appears on the sheet of paper.

Sender: M

Me: M could stand for "Mum" or "Majo". Which one of you is writing me?

Sender: Marie

Me: Majo, is it you? I receive your message with difficulty. This first contact is hard, but I hope that little by little, it will be better. Will you confirm if this is you by a simple yes or no? Thank you. I will wait.

Majo: Yes. Thank you for honouring my memory. I am so happy. I love you all so much.

I love you.

Me: Majo, thank you for your great effort. I am glad you have come into contact by using my humble hand. Thank you for your help and your eternal love. To facilitate this contact, if you are still here, I will ask you questions; you can answer with a simple yes or no. Are you with Viv and Del at this moment? I know you are with me too, but I know you can be at several places at once.

Majo: Yes.

---

68   Majo's daughter Nickname for Delphine.

Me: Where are you all now?

Majo: On the way towards me, my memory.

Me: I receive you better, Majo; it is easier now. Are you happy to see them come to you?

Majo: Very happy. I love them both. What a joy to see them together.

Do not cry, Del. You must always smile. I love you all. Pray. Never be tired of praying.

§§§

Spirit Writings: November 16, 2007; Start Time 9:20 p.m. End Time 11:50 p.m.

Me: "Mum, help me, as I am lost. I have so many dark ideas right now. I am tired of my life. I beg you, please guide me. You know everything. You know the things that stir in my heart. I am completely desperate in this life, of my life. Please help me. Guide me, Mum. I love you.

—N

Mum: Noël, my child, I know your torment. The universe has been working to change everything in your present life. Noël, always listen to what your heart tells you, not the logic of things. We got it all wrong, my children. Peace be in thee, my daughter. Many tests lie further ahead, but keep faith in the universe. I love you very deeply, my child. I love you all. Keep the faith.

§§§

In retrospect, I guess Mum—through Franc—made me start the communication again, as she knew that I was going through a tough time in my life and I was not happy. I was going through difficult times in my marriage. I was fed up with life itself and over everything, and as I was unhappy, I filed for divorce, which I obtained in October 2008. I was working nearly seventy hours and seven days a week; there was not an exact time to finish work I was exhausted, stressed, depressed, and fighting hard to raise my two children and give them everything they needed. I remember the days that I had to work as Data Entry Operator full time, [9:00 a.m. to 5:00 p.m.]. I went straight after to my second job as a Service Cashier [6:00 p.m. to 9:00 p.m.] and after that directly to my third job as a Video Coder at the post office, where I worked until 3:00 a.m. in the Christmas season. I remember falling dead asleep on my keyboard one night. My hands couldn't even type one single letter on the keyboard anymore as I was totally exhausted and out of energy. My body wouldn't respond to any even simple action. I was really overdoing it. I did not eat, but I smoked cigarette after cigarette at each break, thinking about my endless problems: marital, financial, familial, and so on. I did not see my children much. It was sad for me to leave them, but I had no choice. I had to work! I had no social life; I was just a workaholic. No wonder I ended up in a hospital with atrial flutter and fibrillation [abnormal rhythms of the heart]. A cardiologist, psychologist, and psychiatrist treated me, and I ended up in the hospital now with life heart medications and anti-depressants, feeling depressed as I couldn't work. I was underweight and disappearing and as I didn't barely eat something, this is what caused the AF[69]. I felt that my marriage was over and that I had to do something to bring

---

[69]   Atrial Flutter & Fibrillation

back the harmony in our home, as I didn't want the children to experience any more fights between me and my soon-to-be ex-husband. I couldn't stand our lives being upside-down anymore. Therefore, I ended my marriage. Today, my ex-husband and I are best of friends. We both care for our children, and we have a much better relationship than we did when we were married. Illness and stress got the best of us at that time. At last we understood each other, and now we work in harmony for the best interest of our children. We have a mutual respect for each other. In the end, we did not hate each other because I asked for divorce. I know that sometimes, I was not the best wife. He was not the best husband either crying out loud. However, I guess we had our time together and I believe the end of our marriage was meant to be for new things to happen for me. JN,[70] if I offended you by asking for divorce at that time, I am very sorry if I hurt you. In retrospect, therefore, We are free from any hurt or resentment we may have had towards each other.

By the time I filed for divorce and was already separated, I had an affair with Reece.[71] I was not proud of it. For years, I had remorse, but today, I have no more guilt. I did what was best for both of us and our loved ones at that time. Reece will surely recognize himself for all the pain he caused me at that time, as I faced issues without his support and if he doesn't want to do so, God will surely make him remember it when he shall return to the source. Today, I free myself from any resentment towards you, Reece; therefore, I am free of any hate towards you. Likewise, you are free, knowing that I forgive you for all you put me through. I cried over

---

[70]   Nickname for my ex-husband
[71]   Fictitious name

what I had to do at that time as I had no other choice back then, but to this day, I have learned that acknowledging our wrong makes it easier to forgive ourselves. I am free. I have no more remorse.

After my divorce, I met Julien,[72] but it did not lead anywhere. I was very patient, as I wanted this relationship to work between us. However, it did not work out. After several years, I finally had the courage to break up with him and moved on. I free myself from any resentment for Julien as well and set myself free; you are free as well, knowing that everything you did at that particular time is all forgiven.

To my siblings and family, I free myself from any resentments or hate. In so doing, I am free. You are free too, knowing that everything is forgiven from my end.

Always love each person, as life is a school wherein we make mistakes, but we learn from them. We try not to make them again, and we demonstrate love in a much better way. I love you all. We should not have any resentment for each other. We all were meant to have these experiences, so I am grateful that you were all put on my path. The yin and the yang are linked; therefore, both good and bad have to be together too. I learned that we need both to know the difference. I love you all for that.

I think I had an impact on each of your lives, and each one of you impacted on mine as well. I don't regret anything. All was meant to be this way. You brought me what I needed most; which is experiencing the hardest things in life to grow and become a much stronger and better person. Yes, you all helped me to become the new me, so thank you for this. If I had not experienced as much hurt or tribulations,

---

[72] Fictitious name

I would not be the woman I am today. So, yes indeed, I am endlessly grateful for all the bad that happened and all we have been through together. Through you, I learned lessons that I never need to experience again.

I wish you all well.

I am sending you ongoing light and love directly from my heart, now and forever.

§§§

Spirit Writings: January 23, 2008; Start Time 5:39 a.m. End Time 5:59 a.m.

Mum: This magic moment that unites us transcends everything, because when you keep me in your heart, the existing thread of love between you and I increases. Love is fantastic, magical, fairy-like, and inexplicable; the more we love, the more our capacity to love grows.

No space disunites existing love, Noël.

It is a flowery field; it is the sun.

A fragrance turns continuous desire.

It is a gentle caress.

It is a light in the heart.

It is a heat in the soul, and it feels so good, so filled with joy—an inexplicable happiness.

Love, Noël, is continuous sharing.

Continue to cherish, share, and give.

Cultivate love inside, and you will always be filled with happiness beyond explanation.

You have enormous love in you because you are between heaven and earth already.

You exist not only on earth but also in heaven, for you are in communion with me; this, Noël, is proof of love beyond what some beings cannot understand. Send and scatter love always, my child. I love you."

§§§

Spirit Writings: January 27, 2008; Start Time 6:00 a.m. End Time 7:00 a.m.

Me: Hi, dear Mother. It's Noële Aux Quatre Vents. I love you. Do not ever forget that. Thank you for being in my dreams. I experience you every night, Mum. You are present in my heart. I love you. I am also sending you love from all your children, grandchildren, and great-grandchildren. Guide us forever. We still love you and Majo.[73] *Majo, I love you. Always be happy where you are. One day, we will meet again, my loved ones.*

—Noël

Mum: What you sent us is beautiful.

The love that you are feeling is like a bouquet of roses, so we give you our respect, my child. I love you. I will mould you more beautifully; soon, you will work for heaven. Be ready. You are on the road. You already live heavenly purposes down here. You feel the way it can be in heaven. It is many times better, but you will live it on earth, Noël, as well as

---

[73]   Sister in heaven

**in the immensity of heaven. Nothing happens by
chance, because everything is written, Noël.
So, go where your heart tells you to go forever.
Live everything with faith, and remain positive.**

Me: My children[74] embrace you very strongly, Mum.

**Mum: I embrace them in return. Continue to take care
of them, as you have done so well. I am sure they love
you very much, Noël. You are a wonderful mother,
dear. Always share the immensity of your love, and
give without restraint always. Love without limits.
That is how you will experience the joys of heaven.**

*Me: Mum, thank you for coming back to me through Franc[75] to
start the automatic/spirit writings again. I am so happy to
resume it. I feel at peace. It is such a joy. If there had been no
contact with Franc, I would never have started up again. I
was very discouraged that the family did not believe in them
at all and also discouraged with my current life.*

**Mum: The angel to whom I have spoken will find you,
Noël.**

Me: What happened, Mum? Can you tell me more?

Mum: I love him.

*Me: Well, Mum, I see that you cannot tell me more. We will
talk about that in dreams if you do not mind. I love you
and you sure know everything.*

Mum: Yes. Give and receive without getting tired.

*Me: Do you have a message for your children? I will give them
your messages, but I do not know what they will think. I
remain open to any questions they would like to ask you
or what they would like to share with you. Much love*

---

[74]   My two children, Caroline and Loïc

[75]   Franc is a medium from Paris

from your children, Mum. Monique[76] loves reading your
messages.

**Mum: Tell them that I send them all my love, and it
is so great that it spreads across the vastness and
splendour of the universe. I love you all so much.
Believe in yourself—in your hopes, your dreams,
and your deepest desires. I am with you always and
forever, my darling. I love you. Never forget this.**

*Me: We love you too, Mum. I embrace you tightly and hold
you in my arms to give you a tender hug with great love.*

**Mum: Me too, Noël. I gave you enormous hugs recently
and again now.**

Me: Bye, and see you soon, my dear mum.

**Mum: Continue the game of love, for you will not get
tired of it. Continue to wear a beautiful smile on
your lips. I love you. Be happy and thirsty for love
always.**

Me: I love you, Mum.

Mum: I send you all my love. On this day, you will feel it.

Me: Thank you, Mum.

§§§

Spirit Writings: January 30, 2008; Start Time 4:15 a.m. End
Time 4:43 a.m.

*Me: I am here, Mum. I made the effort, despite my heavy sleep,
to be present and faithful to your call. I wish to wake up
easily every time you call me now. I let go of my stress right
now, and I see only the present instant. I will welcome this*

---

76   Monique is my sister, Mum's daughter

new day with much love and tenderness in my little heart.
I love you forever, my beautiful mum.

Mum: Thank you for being here. Your efforts affect me greatly.

Love without measure, restraint, or limitation always, sweetheart.

I love you.

My love is always present and alive in your heart filled with love.

Speak love, make love, and share love every moment that you live your life.

Whatever you do, do it with more love.

There is love in everything God created and in each being, because he created everything with lots of love.

Look at the sun, the sky, the stars, the moon, the earth, the universe, and beauty; feed yourself with their love.

Look at the plants, fields of flowers, mountains, valleys, and oceans, and feed yourself with their splendour and love.

Look around at everything that exists, and feed yourself with their love.

Look at the birds, and feed yourself with their tender example of love.

Feed yourself with all the love you receive from all things, all beings, and live that happiness, my child.

Doesn't music bring you love?

Doesn't writing bring you love?

Doesn't a dream bring you love?

Doesn't a gesture, a gaze, or a word bring you love?

Is not our communication with each other love?

Isn't a sweet and tender thought a form of love?

Everything is wonderful;

Do not look behind you anymore, as it was not lived in love;

What is past, is past; it is no longer.

Look before you, darling, at what you can accomplish and make with love;

Moreover, live only love.

I love you.

Do not ever forget this.

You are in me, and I am in you throughout this immense love, one for the other.

You already understand that you need to feed love, as it dies if you do not take great care of it.

You love me, and I love you. What could be more beautiful, more precious?

I love you all, my darlings. I love you forever. Nothing separates us.

Think about it deeply. This is how you will maintain our love. I love you.

Live peace and love, and give generously.

—Mum

§§§

Spirit Writings: January 31, 2008; Start Time 4:22 a.m. End Time 4:47 a.m.

Me: This is me, Mum, at your call. Here I am. Guide my hand. It is poised and ready. I always adore you and all your grandchildren. I love you very much.

Mum: Noël, it's so beautiful that you're faithful to the call of love. Moreover, our love is eternal. Send all my love to all my children. I love you. Noël, between you and me, there is no time or space, because the desire to meet is there. We find each other when we wish and where we want to in our heart. Never forget this. Nothing can restrain love that already exists. I love you, you love me, and that love will let you do anything. I am glad to find you and to be able to share with you my love for all my darlings. I am fine, and Majo[77] is also.

We embrace you, and we love you and protect you always. Pray. Do not become tired of asking, because everything you ask for with faith will be given to you. Do not despair. We protect all of you and love you. Open your eyes and ears to the wonders that heaven sends you every day and those that already exist. Live in harmony. Share love always.

I offer you my love. I love you. Thanks for being there to meet with me, Noël.

—Mum

Spirit Writings: February 3, 2008; Start Time 10:30 p.m. End Time 10:40 p.m.

Me: Oh, Mum. Sometimes life seems so beautiful and at other times so painful. However, I am not discouraged, Mum. Otherwise, everything would become dark and sad. I will not shed all my tears in handkerchiefs. I will fight, Mum. Pardon my crying tonight. I suffer too much. I do not know

---

[77] My sister with Mum in heaven

why so much pain surrounds me tonight. It took over me suddenly. Pardon me, Mum. I love you. Will I one day be happy, Mum? Why so much anguish and so many concerns? I love you. Please hug me close to your heart, Mum.

I cried too much, so I had to stop temporarily.

§§§

Above Conversation Resumed; Start Time 10:50 p.m. End Time 11:05 p.m.

Me: Mum, excuse this time of weakness on my part. I will fight, Mum. I made you this promise. If you want, use my hand to send me a quick note. I expect you, darling mum. I love you.

Mum: Noël, I bring you my immense love from where I am. I am very close to you at this moment, because I feel your pain deeply. I know it is not easy currently, but believe that happiness is there already.

Me: Thanks for being there, Mum. Thank you for your love. I love you.

I got nothing more that time, but this meant so much to me because it conveys so much love.

§§§

Spirit Writings: February 4, 2008; Start Time 5:30 a.m. End Time 5:35 a.m.

Me: Hello, Mum. Yes, I spent a sleepless night. I did not close my eyes. I do not know why I am in this state. I am afraid that something will happen. Why am I on the alert, Mum? This day will be tough after last night. I love you, Mum. Thank you for always being there, Mum.

—Noël

I didn't receive a message.

Me: Why don't you answer me, Mum? I'm so afraid.

§§§

Spirit Writings: February 5, 2008; Start Time 10:32 p.m. End Time 10:46 p.m.

Me: Mum, You know everything, all my troubles and anxieties. You know everything that makes me sad, and you are aware of my state of total depression now. Help me, Mum. I only have you to rely on. I do not doubt for a moment your love, loyal and great. I know that you would never harm me. Thank you for accepting my love, and thank you for the priceless love that you offer without expecting anything in return. I love you, Mum. I love you more than ever. I send you all my suffering, Mother.

—Noël

Mum: My baby …

Me: Mum, tell me, why are there so many mysteries? You know the pain I suffer. I'm starting to feel worn out. So tell me all, Mum. Warn me.

My tears flowed freely, so I stopped writing.

I know the only reason Mum would stay quiet was that I was so sad that day. I also remember that a man hurt me deeply at that point, but I will not waste my time on the details; it is not worth my time. This man turned me down twice; he may recognize himself. However, as I said, today I am free of all resentment and pain. I am free from my heavy past on earth. Yes, I am completely free.

Chapter 16

MUM'S EIGHTIETH BIRTHDAY IN HEAVEN

Spirit Writings: February 8, 2008; Start Time 7:00 a.m. End Time 7:57 a.m.

This took place on what would have been Mum's eightieth earthly birthday.

I made a drawing with hearts, flowers, and a sun and presented it to Mum like a birthday card. I wrote the following message on it: "Happy Birthday, Mama Dearest. We all love you. Kisses. We all embrace you."

I also sang her favourite song in French "Reviens vers le Bonheur" by an unknown author in the 60's:

> "Reviens vers le bonheur
> Reviens vers l'idéale tendresse
> Ton cœur charme mon coeur
> Je ne peux vivre sans tes caresses
> Même s'ils sont menteurs
> Tes baisers que mes lèvres m'endillent
> Seuls semblent embellir ma vie
> Reviens vers le Bonheur."

Meaning in english:
"Come back to happiness
Come back to the perfect tenderness
Your heart charms my heart
I cannot live without your touch
Although they are lies
Your kisses that my lips beg
Only seem to embellish my life
Come back to happiness."

Me: Mum, on this day, I sing your favourite song because it's your day. Happy birthday, Mum! Five years ago, you entered the bliss of heaven. You are happy where you are. I send you a thousand kisses and thousands of red roses from all of us here. We all love you, your children, grandchildren, and great-grandchildren. We hold you close to our hearts on this beautiful day. I love you, Mum. You are out of sight but close to our hearts. Between you and us, there is no time or space. We don't need to see you, hear you, or feel you to continue to love you in silence in our hearts. As long as we keep you close, nothing will separate us, Mum. No matter the time or distance, we can find each other. It's magical. We want to love well. We want to give love without expecting anything in return—without waiting to see you, hear you, or receive a sign from you. We value knowing in our hearts that you are present and that you love us. Without seeing you, hearing you, touching you, we all love you, Mum. This love is so beautiful, Mum. Just imagine it, and smile, and feel the love we give and receive. It is beyond the imagination, Mum. I love you like that, and it's natural for me to do so. I did not need to see to believe or to love. I love all that is heavenly in nature and in people. I love you, Mum. Happy Birthday, dear Mum. All of your children embrace you.

— Noël

Mum: I love you very dearly. Never forget it. As long as you keep the thread of love, which unites us across time, love will exist between you and me, and our communication will be possible. I am here always to tell you the words of love and reminding you that I guide and protect you. You understood limitless love. Nothing hinders love, as we hold love in the heart, the soul, and the mind. If you keep your love intact, everything is possible, my angel. If you erase the memory in your heart and your mind, it dies.

Love nourishes silently, and you will see that it will continue to grow in you. Do not dwell on unimportant things. Concentrate only on keeping love attached to your heart.

Maintain its life, and it will exist forever. You understand my treasure. I know you understand, because it is what you do now.

Believe and think about happiness, and you will have it, my darling. Convey my love to the whole family. I love you so much. I protect you and surround you with my light. Think of me, and I shall rush to you. Talk to me, and I will hear you. I embrace you and your siblings. Do not be sad on this day. Weep not. Be happy for me and for yourself. I can better assist you from here. Follow heavenly roads always. Peace and happiness be with you always, despite worry and pain. Be filled with the happiness of love always.

§§§

While I made the drawing for Mum, one of Loïc's toys played a song by itself. The game was on the table next to me, and I was very surprised. It made me smile. This was an amazing physical phenomenon, and lots of them continued to happen after that moment. My sister and I will never forget one of these instances. This particular night, I was tuned in and asking Mum if she was near us; I asked her to let us know that she was there. There was a bunch of roses in a vase on the table where we sat, and one of the roses dropped lower as soon as I asked for a sign. My sister was scared to death, as she had never experienced such physical phenomena with spirits. I asked for evidence from Mum again, and a second rose bent over. My sister ran from the room. I wasn't scared at all, as I know spirits can't harm us without our consent. As I always protected myself, I knew nothing could harm me, especially not my mum.

§§§

Mother's Day.

Spirit Writings: May 10, 2008; Start Time 02:15 p.m. End Time 02.30 p.m.

Me : Dear Mum, I love you and don't forget you.
Mum: My child finally you are here!
Me: Forgive me mum, you know my troubles, my discouragements, my fights. Sometime I really don't have any courage. I would like so much a complete change in my life.

Mum : Believe.

Me: I believe in it Mum, I never give up. I only live for that. Better days than those present.

Mum : [blank]

Me: Mum you don't want to answer me?

Mum: [blank]

Me: Ok Mum, it's your mysterious side again … not telling me more …

Mum: Yes you have the power.

Me: What power Mum?

Mum: The power of all.

Me: You are very mysterious Mum today.

Mum: You see me. Mum.

Me: Yes I see you Mum but only in dreams. But I surely would love to see you in real.

Mum: You see me.

Me: When and where do I see you Mum?

Mum: Pay more attention.

Me: Ok Mum, I will pay more attention. I love you.

Mum: Me too.

Me: Happy Mother's Day. Talk to you soon.

Mum: I am always her.

§§§

Inspirational Writing: May 31, 2008, Anne André

"By not keeping their memories in us, they disappear, they die. By not keeping track in us of their living, those that we knew, acquainted with, loved,

it's letting them die gradually in ourselves, eventually washing any memory, any trace of them and eventually they are forgotten and excluded from our lives ... our daily lives.

But by keeping their memory intact, alive, as if they were still with us is to keep them alive in us, their existence, their living

and by keeping them under our eyes is somehow telling them that they have never been forgotten, that they are still loved and that we like to see them and find them again.

At anytime do not erase them from your life, talk to them, share your joys, your sorrows and make them remain alive in a way as if they were still physically there.

In fact they are still there but in a different form.

At anytime have they really left.

Our ears are deaf, our eyes are blind because they are still among us, always present, alive though we doubt their presence. They are all here alive.

Some deny them. Some don't feel them but others yes still feel their presence still among us.

They continue to surround us and it's the mystery of their unconditional and eternal love."

§§§

I dropped the automatic/spirit writings for good as I faced that year several difficult periods in my life: my separation and divorce, my daughter's wild teenage years, financial difficulties and my illness; I was in AF[78] more often, and this affected my life considerably. I couldn't work as much as I had been working the last several years and I was on my own. I broke down, and when this happened,

---

[78]   Atrial Flutter and Atrial Fibrillation (Abnormal rhythm of the heart)

more problems arose. I faced homelessness as the house we have been living in for the last five years was sold and we were asked to move out. I didn't have enough to lodge as much house rental applications as most of them was rejected coz of my poor single income. Churches assisted my children and I with food, furniture and other things we needed. Yes, I had to beg for food near the church and the Salvos.[79] I have known it all. Hanover, a community-based agency, assisted us with a shelter temporarily, but after one month, I was back on my feet again. I challenged myself to get a home to rent again, and I got one immediately. I have always been a motivated woman, whatever the situation I was experiencing. I couldn't work anymore, I was facing financial difficulties, and I was physically and mentally exhausted, but I fought even when I was down on the ground. I slowly got back on my feet again, faced life, and said, "I haven't finished my journey here yet". I regained my confidence and got strength from an unknown source. I was ready for any other challenges that life could send me. I stayed in that new house, renting it as a single mum for another two years and not working due to heart fibrillations. I was never in arrear with my rent. I wasn't rich, but I got food and clothes for my children and continued looking after their education. For me that was all that matters. Life was tough, but it did not kill me. "No, not yet", I said to myself. I survived by making sacrifices. God and all the angels to whom I was praying provided me with everything I needed for my two children and myself. All I needed were brought to me like "mana"[80] from the universe. I provided

---

[79]   Charitable Institution

[80]   Holy Bread

my two children with everything they needed. I remained positive, and I knew deep down that I was going to succeed. I was well guided by a higher force and trusted my guts to do such and such and I threw myself into the challenges. The "never give up" mentality was in return very well paid and my prayers were all answered as heaven sent me several windfalls, and with all the money I received, I invested in a new house, which I bought in May 2013. God, thank you for everything. Through all the experiences and the challenges, I never gave up. Now, I am overwhelmed by so much blessings, and I am so grateful for my house and my new life. My daughter, about to turn twenty-one, turned out to be an amazing woman, and my son is turning fifteen soon. I'm so proud of what I have accomplished for them, and I hope that one day they will remember me, as I always remember and love my mum still. I hope that they will proudly talk about me to their children and say that I was a strong woman, like their grandmother. I've made mistakes, and I certainly wasn't a saint, as I had to do the things that were best for me, my children, my ex-husband, and those concerned and their loved ones at that particular time. I had plenty of remorse for what I did until some angels told me not to in a dream. They said that I did what I had to do at that specific time, and I did it for everyone's good. They told me not to look back but to look forward and to change my life positively, which I did. Today, I live in a beautiful house surrounded by hundreds of angels. I know that they protect our home and us inside of it. I had a very tough life from a very young age, but now, finally, I'm resting and enjoying life to the fullest. I will do this until I get to the other side, where I belong. I am no longer the old version of myself. I learned through all the experiences, good and bad, which made me the new person I am proud to be today.

§§§

In 2010, I was drawn to a particular DVD at a public library. This movie, *Conversations with God*, based on a book series by Neale Donald Walsch, changed my life completely. After watching the movie, I read the first three books of the fifteen-book series of the same title. I am 100 per cent certain that my guardian angel or spirit guides drew my attention to that movie to change my life completely. I met a fantastic medium named Joanne King[81] at one of her psychic and mediumship sessions at Patterson Lakes Community Centre, in September 2013, and this meeting again impacted on my life. She told me that she saw not one but two books on top of my head. I was shocked. Until that time, my manuscript was still in a suitcase, and no one knew about it but my siblings. If I hadn't met Joanne, I guess this book would never have been published. Franc, the French medium, told me to publish my book in 2007, and I didn't hear this advice from Joanne until six years later. I had to do something. This would be my last chance to reveal all the messages Mum sent from the other side and prove to the world that nothing ever dies. And I'm sure that through these mediums Mum was still sending me the message to publish these letters. After physical death, there is another form of life: a spiritual, religious, conscious, life. You can call it whatever you prefer, but the point is that there is life

---

[81]   My current psychic medium Joanne King, author of *Nobody Will Ever Believe You*.

after physical death. In fact I would call it "life after life," as in reality, we never die. We are pure energy, and energy never dies. In January 2014, I decided to put together all the messages to publish this book. I guess I still feared of the reaction of my siblings and family in general, so I put the project back in its case. I knew that I was doing the wrong thing, but in fact, I think it was meant to be published this year in 2015, as the universe waited for the right moment to make it happen. At the end of 2014, I was guided again to contact the same first publisher I contacted one year earlier. I went back to my first choice of publisher and signed the contract for the submission of my manuscript. "There is no turning back", I said to myself.

Now, all I need to do is watch and see, and let the magic happen. If it is a big success, I will translate it into French and publish it in French-speaking countries as well. All I wish is that the more people possible on this earth to read mum's letters from heaven. For me, it's not really the profits that matters but the amount of souls it's going to touch and lives it's going to change to the better. To all my angels, archangels, higher masters, spirit guides, and my guardian angel, thank you so much for your guidance throughout my journey. Thank you for making it achievable for all to read this and share in the light, the love, and the name of the Father, the Son, and the Holy Spirit. Amen

Chapter 17

A NEW MESSENGER—MY SPIRIT GUIDE

Spirit Writings: 02 November 2013, Start Time 10:20 a.m.
End Time 10.35 a.m.

I tried automatic/spirit writings again after five years. I really didn't know what to expect. To my big surprise, I was no longer in communication with my mum. Instead, my spirit guide was there. I'm still new to mediumship abilities (clairvoyance, clairaudience, and clairsentience). I will not say I can predict your future, bring over your money, I'm really not into this. No, I am more someone who will tune in with whatever "up there" wants to deliver to you through me. I joined a circle to train and develop my psychic gifts to recognize messages from beyond more easily. After a while, I stopped going to the circle, as I felt called to other purposes. I don't know yet what they are, but I have lots of inspirational writings, so maybe I was born to write many books. I truly think that I am clairsentient, clairaudient, and clairvoyant, as I can sense, hear, and see things with increasing ease. I see forms, auras, colours, and sparkles of light, and I have vivid dreams as well as I hear soft voices whispering me words or phrases. I guess I have an inspirational writing gift that is part of my mental mediumship and I love researching, reading and learning more and more about communications with the angels, archangels and higher masters and other. I remain open to whatever the spirit world has to bring me, as I feel there is more to come. I had a fascinating experience at a trance workshop. My medium, Joanne King, went into a trance, and something transfigured her; without a doubt, I saw my mum in front of me for a couple of seconds. I was petrified, but it was an amazing feeling to see her again after so many years. I had chills all over my body. It was really an amazing experience. I would love to be a Trance Medium. Oh my Lord, the heaven on earth I am living is so amazingly beautiful.

My spirit guide dictated things for me to write.

I saw a picture of a cruise boat in my mind. Maybe it was to let me know that I will go on a boat cruise to experience something. That would be wonderful, as I have always wanted to go on a Pacific Island cruise.

The spirit guide also inspired the following words:

Just follow your path.
You will see things soon.
Don't be afraid.
We are here to help always.
Just follow your instincts; listen to us in your heart.
Continue your journey –
Lots and lots of meditation.
Fasting is necessary.

Detach from the physical demands.
Elevate to spiritual awareness.
Don't you worry, child.
God has plans for you.
We are here to help you make it happen.
Just open your door and let us in.
Meditation is good. Pray, and pray harder. Talk to us;
we are the lights.
Don't be afraid: your awareness is taking a new direction
towards us. You are climbing the stairs to us. We will
make things happen easily on your journey. Your yes is
an affirmation that you want God in your life, and we
will be always around you, to guide you to make the
right choices for you and all your loved ones.
We all send blessings. We are always nearby,
So don't hesitate to call upon us.

—Your spirit guide

I'm not sure yet whom these communications are from, but I got these words just after meditating and seeing the colours purple and green. I see these two colours each time I close my eyes. I felt healed by higher energies and felt like there was a hand on each of my ears. This experience was wonderful, and I can't describe the heavenly state to which it brought me. I think I was in a trance state. I felt so good.

§§§

Spirit Writings: December 13, 2013; Start Time 2:05 a.m. End Time 2:30 a.m.

A voice in my head said, "Anne, wake up."

Therefore, I woke up and opened my laptop, and this is the message my mind received.

"Wake up, Anne. Wake up. We need the world to be ready for the coming of our lord Jesus. Thank you for listening when we call. We need everyone to listen and work in accordance with us; we are here to help you in every way. You don't need to be afraid; we are the food and the light. It's important that you understand this; you need to trust us—trust our guidance. Be awake and ready to listen to us. We are your spiritual guides, the voices that guide you on the right path towards new developments. Humankind has to change its attitude towards the impossible; we are the impossible that happens each time you call us. We are nearby and here to guide you always; listen and pay attention when we talk to you in your mind and your heart; whatever you hear in your mind, we are talking to you there. Pay attention and continue persevere in your development to the higher spiritual level. God is love, and love is God, and you are God, and God is you and I. All of us are one in God, and God is in us all; you must understand that, and the world needs to understand and accept it in each living being. Do not judge or point fingers. God is in everyone, and in everyone, we love God. God is in each living being, everywhere around you. We are around you everywhere too; we are here to help you ascend to the higher pathways. Love, love, love is all that matters; forgive and love repeatedly. Wipe away any issue and start again with love; start each day as if you wiped your memory of the day before. If you don't remember anything, what would you do? Love each other as if

you didn't remember any anger, hate, or resentment from yesterday or the past. Start a new day—a new beginning—with love. If you get this right, you will understand that life itself is love. Each day do everything with love; say everything with love. Every moment should be filled with love; surround yourself with love, and you will discover the changes and the magic that happens. Act like a newborn who smiles at everyone without distinguishing between people. When you were born, you were ready to love without judging any racial group, language, religious background, belief, sexual orientation, gender identity, ethnic background, skin colour, or nationality. There was no barrier. You were not born knowing discrimination. When you grew up, someone taught you what to think, and you developed bad feelings towards other religions, races, ethnicities, and so forth. They taught you wrong, dear ones. You got us all wrong, and you got God all wrong. God loves everyone, and so do we. We love all races, religions, and ethnic backgrounds. For us, there is no difference as we are all one. It's time to change your perception of things from now on, if you got this all wrong. However, don't have any bad feelings in your heart or think about what happened in the past. Don't keep replaying what happened in the past; there is no point for to go there; what is done is in the past. What you do with love today, in the love of Jesus Christ, is important. Remember this always, and you will find true happiness. True happiness is in your heart, but you have to choose it and live it. If your day is full of joy, happiness, and love, it will change your life completely. You will give and receive an abundance of love. This Christmas season, share your love with others: a smile, a helping hand, or a kind word is a little gesture of love. You can make a difference, and you can be a messenger of love. Be love; do love; live love. Thank you for listening. We love you. Trust us, your spiritual guides.

§§§

Spirit Writings: December 13, 2013; Start Time 2:05 a.m. End Time 2:30 a.m.

Before I lost the connection, I asked my spirit guide to give me a message for everyone, and here is what I got:

Dear loved ones, be reassured that we are always here for you. We are your guides, your daily bread, feeding you with spiritual thoughts. Just call upon us, and we will arrive to help; don't hesitate if you are in doubt of anything. Call upon us, and we will help you get on the right path. Spiritual means light, which means guidance, which means holiness; whether or not you believe in the Almighty, spirituality is the Almighty—it is God itself. We are made in God's image. Therefore, God is all of us together. We are one in God, and God is in all of us. Never doubt whether God hears when you ask; he always hears you and is always ready to give you whatever you need, so just ask, and you shall receive.

Dear ones, you are doing the right thing here together. We need you to work harder to prove that there is a hereafter and that we live on eternally. There is no death. We all survive death on earth, and we live on, doing what we used to do. So, be certain that we

work hard too, and we never stop. We always send you messages, but most of the time, you don't hear us; you just don't listen or come to meet us. However, we are not discouraged, and we pursue our work to get your attention. Thank you for finally hearing us, feeling us, and seeing us; some of you are doing such great work with the sceptics. Trust and believe, and don't give up in your determination to know more about our existence. Yes, there is life, and everything goes according to plan. We work as a team with you; thank you for making the effort of seeing, hearing, meeting, and feeling us. You are doing a great work. Keep going and keep following our guidance.

There is life, yes, as none of us dies. Everything and everyone has its place here. Be good, and do well, and you too shall be in a wonderful place.

Thank you for listening.

Love, love, and love,

Your spirit guide

I dreamed of Archangel Michael after this message, and I saw him clearly for five seconds in a clear vision. Royal blue and purple surrounded him, and he was magnificently beautiful. I woke up suddenly after the vision, and he was still in my head. I saw him in front of my bed while awake, and I knew that he was the one who sent me the most recent messages. Yes, they were all from Archangel Michael.[82]

---

[82] Michael was known as a healing angel and then, over time, he was called a protector and the leader of the army of God against the forces of evil.

I was supposed to publish this book several months ago, but I experienced a new illness, hips and spine osteoarthritis. I had this condition for my whole life, in fact I was born with several bones abnormalities but I never knew about it. In May 2014, I was very sick. I was in and out of the emergency room and limping so much that I could not take care of any home duties. I was glued to my bed for nearly one month. I heard the harsh news that I would have to undergo a very complex surgery which was to have a Total Left Hip Replacement. I thought I had to face this surgery and a long rehabilitation, and I would need to put this book aside. I didn't know when I would have another chance to get it published, now that I was facing these health issues. However, my surgeon told me that I was too young for surgery; they wouldn't touch me until I was much older. I was relieved and happy. Instead, they treated me with physiotherapy, hydrotherapy, painkillers, nonsteroidal anti-inflammatory drugs and steroid injections to make my daily living smooth and pain free. When I was diagnosed, I swore to myself that I was going to enjoy life to the fullest. I promised myself that I would sing and dance, and this is what I am doing. By the power of healing, I am positive that I will heal myself. To this day, I am back on my feet as if I hadn't been ill with this issue—as if the universe is telling me again, "Anne, you are safe. Go, publish that book!" This is the right time to share it with the world. After twelve years, it is finally here, Mum. The entire world will see your messages. I love you now and forever. Without you, this would not exist. All your attempts to make me understand that you wanted me to publish it finally succeeded. And here it is Mum, proudly to you.

Your humble daughter,

Anne Noëlette André

We are spirits having a physical experience,
Not physical beings having a spiritual experience.
We are light and consciousness returning home.

Now I know that this book needed to be published this year, and I know that the universe, with all its light energies, angels, archangels, spirit and master guides and a higher power force all worked together to make it happen.

I was still working on this book beginning of this year and one of my close siblings had a stroke. After several months in hospital and clinic she is still fighting for recovery of her total right side paralysis. I have a surgery to undergo in my uterus and my son is waiting for his surgery [arthroscopy of his left hip] as well. And my daughter [after CT scan] has been confirmed to only have ONE KIDNEY since birth. Moreover I'm update clued to my bed again due to DDS [Degenerative Disc Desease] in my spine. But it's life and as long as there is life, we need to live it with the right attitude and surrounded by positive energies in order to heal. Good continuation. God Bless. Sending you lots of blessings.

Divine love and light,

Anne Noëlette André

Samples of Mum's Letters
Originals in French

amour et éternel amour de Jésus Christ
de Marie, du Père, fils et Saint Esprit et un seul corps. Nous te
promettons maman de charger de vie et de nous entraîner au mieux car
nous voulons tous te retrouver, ton amour maternel et inégalable ...
que maman ... je l'avoue de notre Seigneur Jésus qui est toujours
notre seul et unique dieu. Sois heureux toujours là où tu es
maman, nous sommes tous vraiment contents que tu aies pu
regarder la maison du Seigneur.

erci de venir à notre rencontre. Je suis heureuse de te voir si sereine. Continue à suivre le

iteras que DES FRUITS et en abondance.

us ma protection tous et mon amour pour vous ne finira jamais. Vivez le CADEAU

ut votre AMOUR EN RETOUR.

devant aucune épreuve, même la pire et plus difficile soit-elle, POU

h'hésitez pas à agir pour DIEU en toute circonstance, même la plus hu

EST INFINI POUR NOUS TOUS.

nais et il est JUSTE et MISÉRICORDE envers nous tous.

NTE de parler en son nom et proclamez sa BONTÉ toujours.

Fin 19:00

Gerda , votre maman pour toujours....

MUM LOVED PRAYING.

Mum's favorite song she enjoyed singing in French at each party occasion.

"Qu'est-ce qu'on attend pour être heureux?
Qu'est-ce qu'on attend pour faire la fête?
Y a des violettes
Tant qu'on en veut
Y a des raisins, des rouges, des blancs, des bleus,
Les papillons s'en vont par deux
Et le mille-pattes met ses chaussettes,
Les alouettes
Se font des aveux,
Qu'est-ce qu'on attend
Qu'est-ce qu'on attend
Qu'est-ce qu'on attend pour être heureux?

Author [Ray Ventura et ses Collégiens – 1938]

About the Author

Anne Noëlette André, previously known as Anne Noëlette André-St Louis, was born on the 21 September 1967 in Mauritius. The Republic of Mauritius is an island nation in the Indian Ocean about 2,000 kilometres (1,200 miles) off the southeast coast of the African continent. The country is multi-ethnic and multicultural; most Mauritians are multilingual and Anne learn to speak and write English, French, Creole over there.

The author came from a family of ten siblings, two of which died at young age before her own birth. She had a difficult childhood and teenage years as experienced stress witnessing difficult times within her family. She married Louis Jean Noël St Louis in 1993. Two lovely children were born from this union though, Mary Rosa Caroline St Louis in 1994 and Michaël Loïc St Louis in 2000. She lost her dad, Pierre Antoine André in 2000, her mum, Daisy Gerda André, in 2003 and her eldest sister, Marie Josée Rave, in 2005 [only two months after the former immigrated to Australia]. Soon after her mum passed over, one of her dearest relative fell seriously ill in the same year which afflicted her more.

Her mum, Daisy Gerda always loved writing letters to all and the author always loved literature. She started conversations with her mum via automatic/writings exactly one month after she passed over. The last conversation was on May 10, 2008 [Mother's Day]. She divorced in Oct 2008 after fifteen years of marriage, as she didn't want her two children to go through what she had experienced as a child. She took full custody and lived as a single mum. Anne has experienced homelessness, financial crisis, hunger and severe depression. She was killing herself to make a living for herself and her two children, and also faced severe health issues in 2010 and had to resign work.

During a phone conversation in 2008, a medium from Paris named Franc [Friend of Anne's sister Monique] told Anne that her mum wanted her to publish the book, but she still hesitated. Eventually, she watched a movie by Neale Donald Walsh titled *Conversations with God,* and a revelation from Joanne King (Anne's personal medium) told her that she will publish not one but two books in a period of two years. Anne decided in January 2014 that she was to write the book finally, as the time was now or never. All the messages from her mum are originally in French.